MICKEY BAKER'S *complete course in* JAZZ GUITAR

CONTENTS

Part I

Part II

PART ONE

LESSON 1

First we shall work with chords. Chords are very important to a jazz musician. The old style of strumming chords for guitar will never do in modern playing, so we will have to work out a complete system. With this style of chords you will learn to play chord solos, make all kinds of introductions, play background for horn players, and all kinds of tricky fillins.

Below you have 26 chords which you must learn to use right away. There are more chords to learn, but these are the most important. We have to limit ourselves to the most important chords, because, as you know, there are so many meaningless chords for guitar that this has to be done.

For your first lesson you are to just study them, "you know," try to finger them, learn names of them, and so on. If you will notice, some of these chords are designed for the key of G major and some for C major. These are the two keys that we are going to work with first. From these keys we will transpose to all of the other keys.

It is very important that everything in the book be transposed to all of the other keys. You should be able to play any song in any key by the time you finish this book, and learning to transpose is the only thing that can help you to do this.

Get a music writing book, and write everything in it for retaining as you go on.

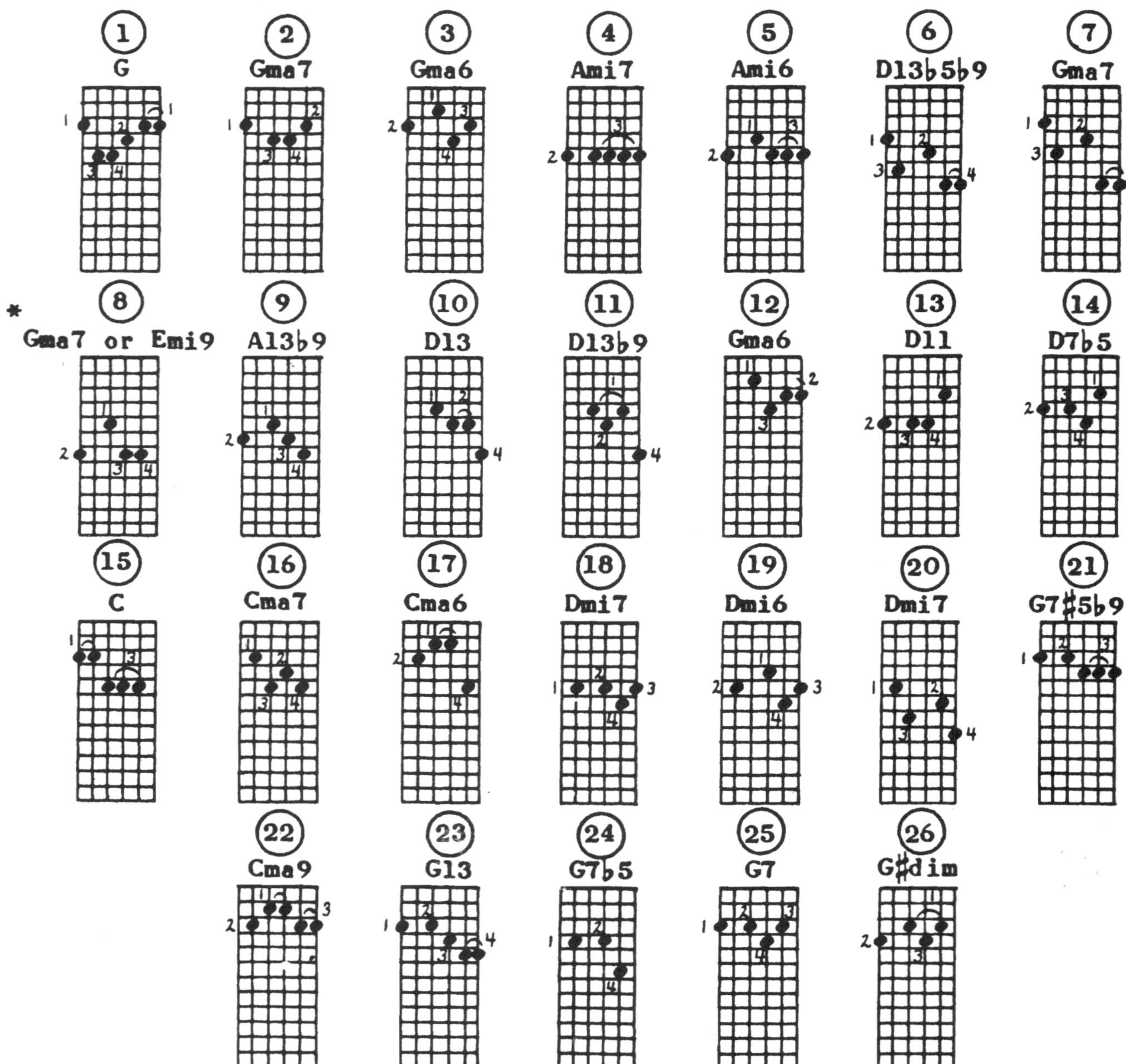

*Some chords have two names, but this will be explained later.

LESSON 2

Now we shall go into Chord Exercises.

Take your G Chords which are the first three chords in Lesson One, and practice them chromatically always up the neck of your guitar as shown below.

CHORDS 1, 2 And 3

G Gma7 Gma6 Gma7 Ab Abma7 Abma6 Abma7 up to Eb Ebma7 Ebma6 Ebma7

CHORDS 2 And 3

Gma7 Gma6 Abma7 Abma6 Ama7 Ama6 up to Ebma7 Ebma6

CHORDS 4 And 5

Ami7 Ami6 Bbmi7 Bbmi6 Bmi7 Bmi6 up to Fmi7 Fmi6

Now We Combine Chords 2, 3, 4 And 5

Gma7 Gma6 Ami7 Ami6 Abma7 Abma6 Bbmi7 Bbmi6 up to Cma7 Cma6 Dmi7 Dmi6

With Chords 4, 5 And 6

Ami7 Ami6 Ami7 D13 b5b9 Bbmi7 Bbmi6 Bbmi7 Eb13 b5b9 up to Fmi7 Fmi6 Fmi7 Bb13 b5b9

Now With Chords 2, 4, 6 And 9

Gma7 A13b9 Ami7 D13 b5b9 Abma7 Bb13b9 Bbm7 Eb13 b5b9 up to Cma7 D13b9 Dmi7 G13 b5b9

LESSON 3

Now that you have a general idea of how the Chords should sound, let's put them to a little work.

First, I'm going to write out the standard changes as they are in some songs, and below them I will write the new ones, the way they should be played against the old ones.

By the way, you are only using Chords No. 1, 2, 3, 4, 5, 6 for these Exercises. Just transpose them to the proper keys.

Standard	G	Gmi	G	Gdim	Ami	D7	G Gdim	Ami D7
New	Gma7 Gma6	Gmi7 Gmi6	Gma7 Gma6	Bmi7 B♭mi7	Ami7 Ami6	Ami7 D13 ♭5♭9	Gma7 B♭mi7	Ami7 D13 ♭5♭9

Standard	B♭mi E♭7	B♭mi E♭7	A♭ A♭6	A♭ A♭6	B♭mi E♭7	B♭mi E♭7	A♭ A♭6	A♭
New	B♭mi7 B♭mi6	B♭mi7 E♭13 ♭5♭9	A♭ma7 A♭ma6	%	B♭mi7 B♭mi6	B♭mi7 E♭13 ♭5♭9	A♭ma7 A♭ma6	%

Standard	Ami	E7	Am	%	E♭7	%	Am	D7
New	Ami7 Ami6	Bmi7 Bmi6	Ami7 Ami6	%	B♭mi7 B♭mi6	%	Ami7 Ami6	Ami7 D13 ♭5♭9

Standard	C7	%	%	%	F	%	%	F♯dim
New	Gmi7 Gmi6	%	%	Gmi7 C13 ♭5♭9	Fma7 Gmi7	Ami7 Gmi7	Fma7 Gmi7	Ami7 A♭mi7

Standard	B♭	%	C7	%	F7	%	B♭	F7
New	B♭ma7 B♭ma6	%	Gmi7 Gmi6	%	Cmi7 Cmi6	Cmi7 F13 ♭5♭9	B♭ma7 D♭mi7	Cmi7 F13 ♭5♭9

LESSON 4

Before I take you into Lesson 4, I want to remind you that every lesson in this book is important, (so you are not to skip anything!!). Give every Exercise all the study you can.

In Lesson 3 you had Chord Exercises in the key of F, G, A♭ and B♭. The six chords that we used for those four keys are the most important Rhythm Chords in these keys.

In Lesson 4 we are going to work out examples on how to use these new chords in place of the standards. We are still using Chords No. 1 to 6.

This will be done the same way as in Lesson 3.

On the top line will be the Standard Chords and on the bottom line, the best way to use the new ones.

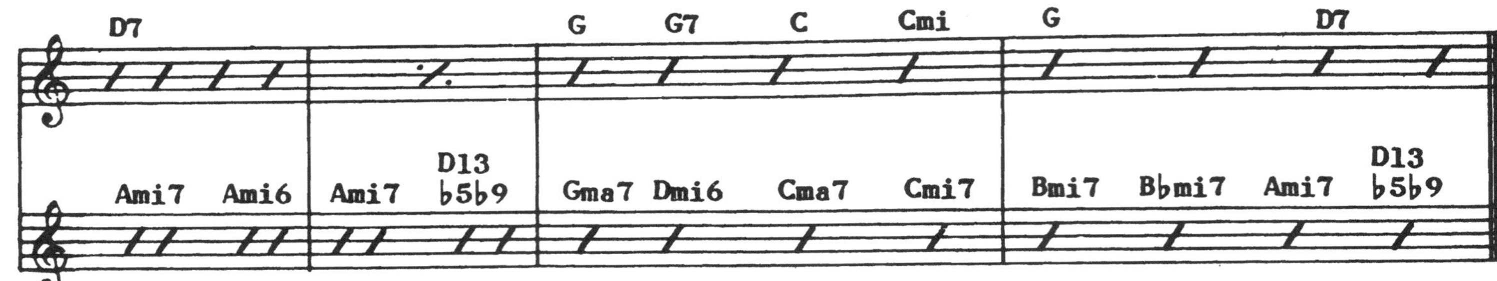

LESSON 5

Now that you have mastered Lesson No. 4 this fifth lesson should be easy. You are to make similar examples of Lesson No. 4.

In the keys of F, A♭ and B♭ major, simply take three pieces of manuscript paper, and transpose Lesson No. 4 to each key. After you have done this and you are sure that they are right, practice each example until you know them all by heart in each key.

Take your time and don't rush through them, this is very important!

LESSON 6

Now for melody chord progressions.

We are still working in the keys of F, G, A♭ and B♭. We will work with the keys of C, D♭ and E♭ later.

Let's work on simple introductions first. Try these examples in G major. You may find some of these very hard to play, but if you practice them chromatically up and down the finger board you will soon become accustomed to them.

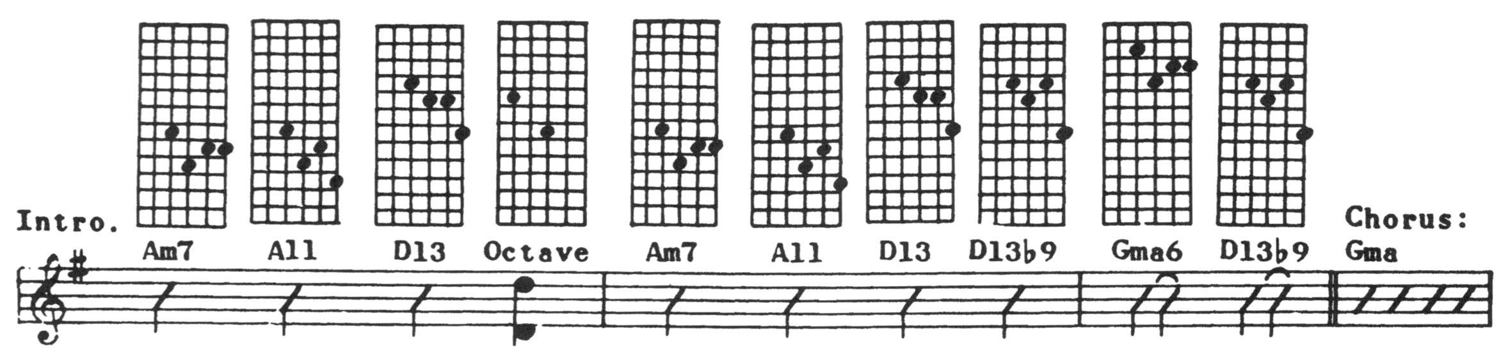

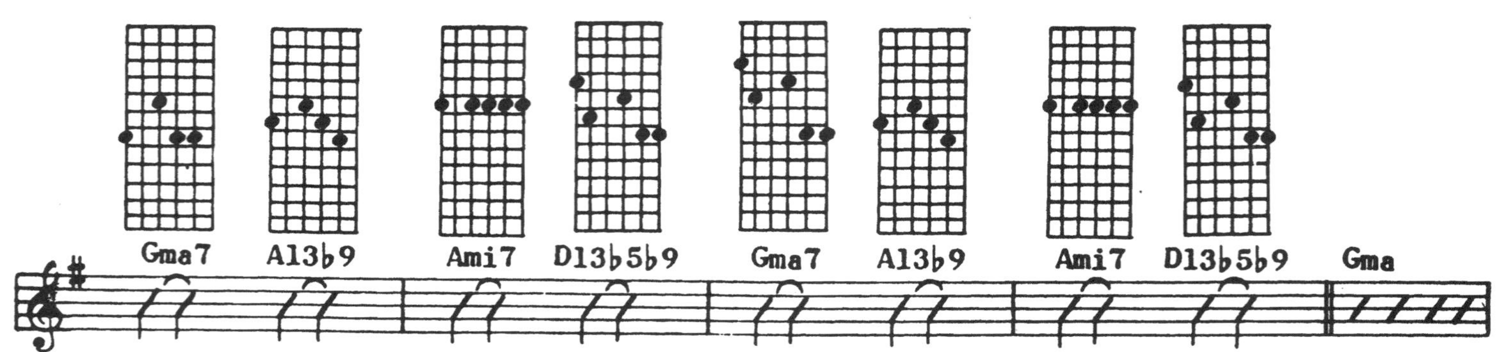

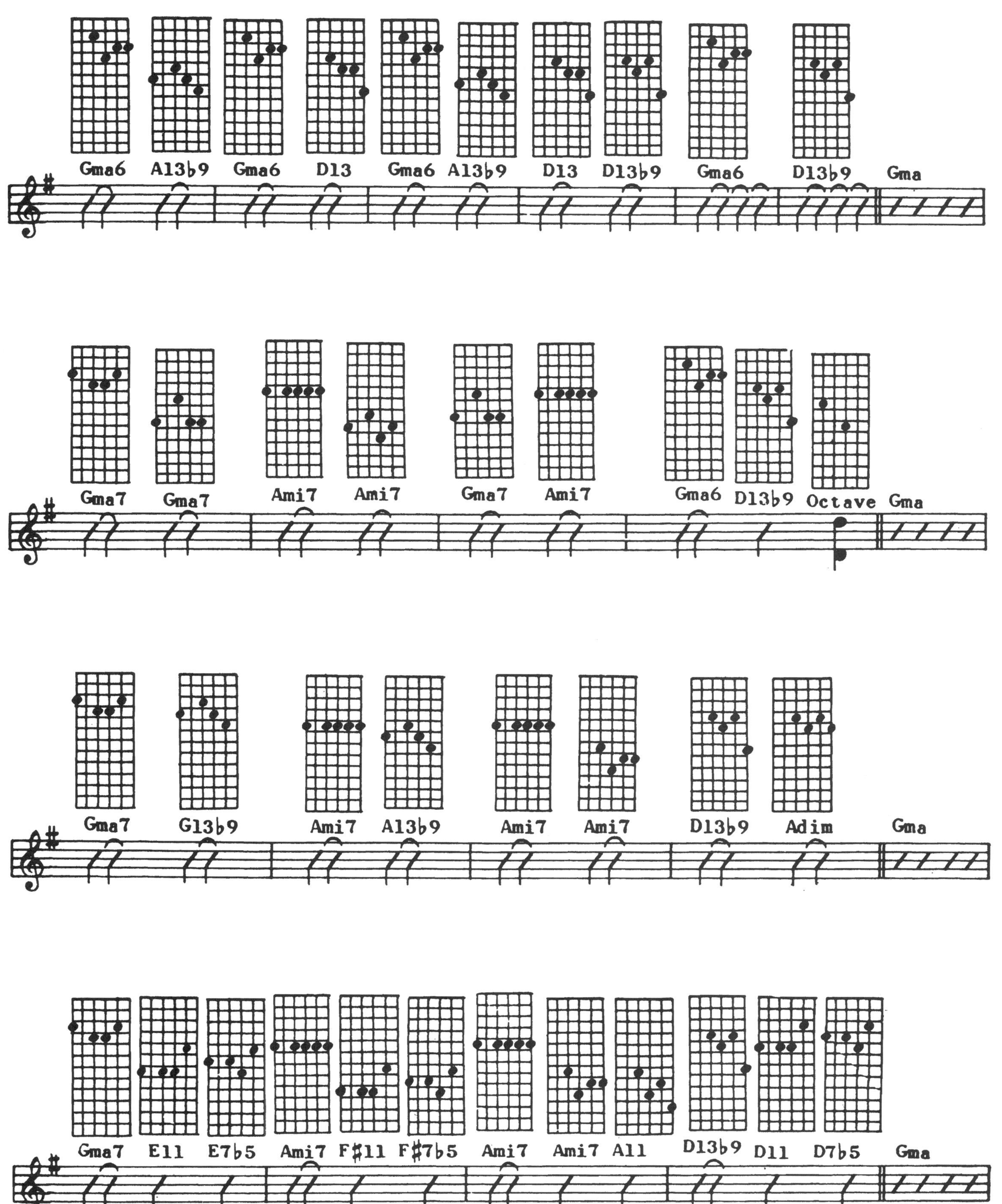
Gma6
A13♭9
Gma6
D13
Gma6
A13♭9
D13
D13♭9
Gma6
D13♭9
Gma
Gma7
Gma7
Ami7
Ami7
Gma7
Ami7
Gma6
D13♭9
Octave
Gma
Gma7
G13♭9
Ami7
A13♭9
Ami7
Ami7
D13♭9
Adim
Gma
Gma7
E11
E7♭5
Ami7
F♯11
F♯7♭5
Ami7
Ami7
A11
D13♭9
D11
D7♭5
Gma

LESSON 7

After you have mastered these examples in G, you are to write out similar examples in the keys of: F, A♭ and B♭. Then practice them in all four of these keys until you can feel comfortable playing them.

Another thing you must do, is to try making other intro's by changing these around in as many ways as you can. This may not be so easy at first, but if you devote enough time to it, you will find yourself making all kinds of intro's from these few chords.

They are your most important melody chords for these four keys. So give them all the attention you possibly can.

Another way to get new ideas is to change the rhythm of the introduction. Try playing them in apreggio style, or try playing the bottom note of the chord first, then the chord.

Use every trick that you can think of to develop new ideas.

LESSON 8

In this Lesson I have a few ideas on how to use the Arpeggio, and the string bass.

Using Introduction No. 2 in Lesson No. 6 work them out and try to make up new ones.

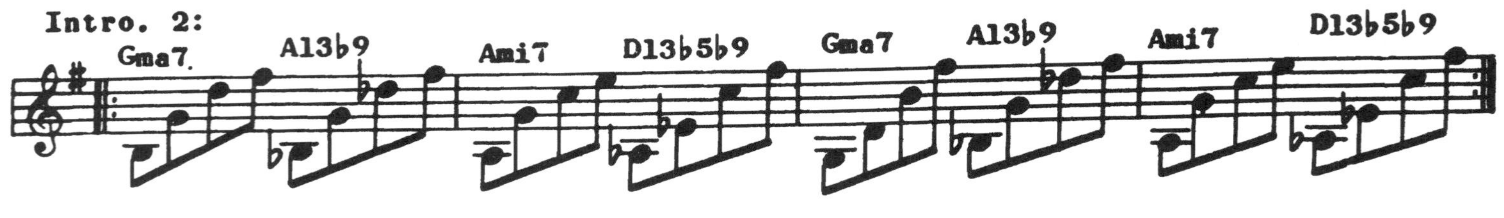

LESSON 9

Now, we come to Chords in the key of C, D♭ and E♭ Major. I do hope that you have followed my instructions to the letter up until now, because if you don't understand your lessons from one to seven, you surely won't understand these lessons to follow.

Just to make sure, revue all of your work up to Lesson No. 8, and make double sure that you have done every lesson as I have told you to do.

First, we will work out Chord Exercises as we did in Lesson No. 2. These exercises are to be worked always up and down the finger board, just as you have done with all of the other chords.

Chords No. 15, 16 And 17

C Cma7	Cma6 Cma7	D♭ D♭ma7	D♭ma6 D♭ma7	up to	G Gma7	Gma6 Gma7

Chords No. 16 And 17

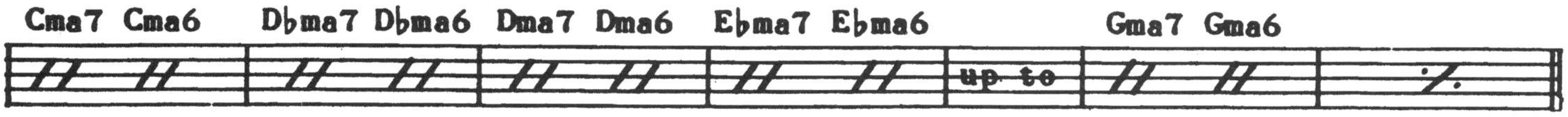

Cma7 Cma6	D♭ma7 D♭ma6	Dma7 Dma6	E♭ma7 E♭ma6	up to	Gma7 Gma6	٪

Chords No. 18 And 19

Dmi7 Dmi6	E♭mi7 E♭mi6	Emi7 Emi6	Fmi7 Fmi6	up to	Ami7 Ami6	٪

Chords No. 16, 17, 18 And 19

Cma7 Cma6	Dmi7 Dmi6	D♭ma7 D♭ma6	E♭mi7 E♭mi6	up to	Gma7 Gma6	Ami7 Ami6

Chords No. 16, 21 And 18

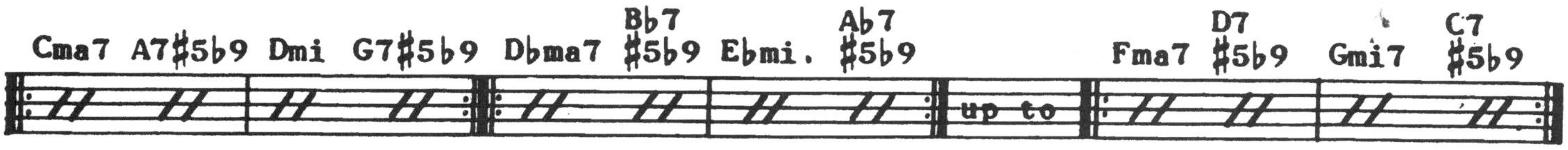

Cma7 A7♯5♭9	Dmi G7♯5♭9	D♭ma7 B♭7♯5♭9	E♭mi. A♭7♯5♭9	up to	Fma7 D7♯5♭9	Gmi7 C7♯5♭9

Chords No. 18, 21 And 22

Dmi7 G7♯5♭9	Cma9 G7♯5♭9	E♭mi7 A♭7♯5♭9	D♭ma9 A♭7♯5♭9	up to	Gmi7 C7♯5♭9	Fma9 C7♯5♭9

LESSON 10

In this Lesson we are going to work on the harmonic structure of these chords. You know, of course, that this is not a course in harmony, but I feel it my duty to give you a little better understanding of how to use these chords.

Now then, any chord on a major mode can be used in place of the major triad.

Let's say that you have one bar of C major, or even two bars:—

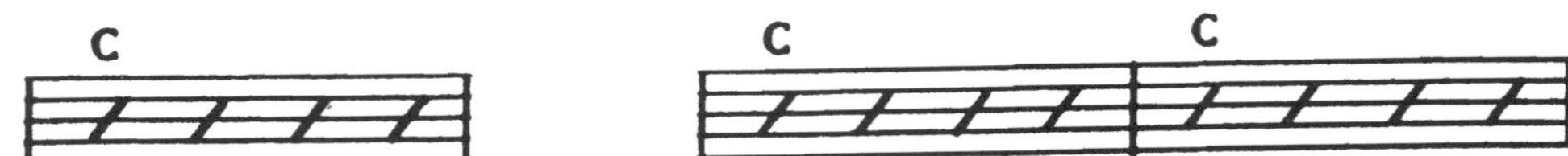

We don't want to strum a C major chord for the whole two bars, because it doesn't have enough color, and besides it sounds corny, so we add color by using progressions that are adaptable as follows:—

In most all cases these progressions are adaptable. The same thing is true with the minor and dominant chords. Such as, if you have a Dmi chord (Any minor chord can be used on the minor mode) Dmi6, Dmi7 and Dmi9 are adaptable, because they are all on the same mode. With dominant chords there is no limit to what can be done. For instance if you have a G7 Chord — you could use G13, G9, G7♯5♭9, G13♯5♭9, G7♯5, G11, G13♭9 and so on. It all depends on how the chords are progressing. You just can't throw these chords in any place; they have to be part of some kind of progression. In the lessons that follow I have written as many chord progressions that are needed to teach you how to use these new chords. They are all in the key of C major. I want you to study them until you know them by heart.

This can't be done overnight. It took me years to figure them out, so it should take you at least two or three months to learn them in the key of C major alone.

LESSON 11
CHORD PROGRESSING

The circled number over each chord indicates which chord is to be used.

(See Lesson 1)

Standard

C | C | C | C

New

(15) C (16) Cma7 | (17) Cma6 (16) Cma7 | (16) Cma7 (17) Cma6 | (1) C (2) Cma7 | (3) Cma6 (2) Cma7 | (2) Cma7 (3) Cma6

C G7 C Dmi G7 C Gdim Dmi G+7

(16) (18) (18) (23) (16) (4) (18) (23) (18) (18) (21)
Cma7 Emi7 E♭mi7 Dmi7 G13 Cma7 Ami7 Dmi7 G13 Emi7 E♭mi7 Dmi7 G7♯5♭9

(2) (3) (4) (5) (2) (4) (4) (6) (4) (4) (6)
Cma7 Cma6 Dmi7 Dmi6 Cma7 E♭mi7 Dmi7 G13♭5♭9 Emi7 E♭mi7 Dmi7 G13♭5♭9

C D7 G7 C C A7 Dmi G7

(16) (17) (4) (5) (18) (21) (16) (17) (16) (17) (18) (21) (18) (23) (18) (21)
Cma7 Cma6 Ami7 Ami6 Dmi7 G13 ♯5♭9 Cma7 Cma6 Cma7 Cma6 Emi7 A7 ♯5♭9 Dmi7 G13 Dmi7 G7 ♯5♭9

(2) (3) (18) (23) (4) (6) (2) (3) (2) (3) (4) (5) (4) (5) (4) (6)
Cma7 Cma6 Ami7 D13 Dmi7 G13 ♭5♭9 Cma7 Cma6 Cma7 Cma6 Emi7 Emi6 Dmi7 Dmi6 Dmi7 G13 ♭5♭9

C E7 Ami Fmi C C7 F Fmi

(16) (17) (4) (5) (4) (5) (4) (5) (16) (17) (4) (6) (2) (3) (4) (5)
Cma7 Cma6 Bmi7 Bmi6 Ami7 Ami6 Fmi7 Fmi6 Cma7 Cma6 Gmi7 C13 ♭5♭9 Fma7 Fma6 Fmi7 Fmi6

(2) (3) (4) (5) (18) (19) (18) (19) (2) (3) (25) (21) (16) (17) (18) (19)
Cma7 Cma6 Bmi7 Bmi6 Ami7 Ami6 Fmi7 Fmi6 Cma7 Cma6 C7 C7♯5♭9 Fma7 Fma6 Fmi7 Fmi6

Practice each of these examples a dozen times a day.

LESSON 12

You see that I have one line for standard chords and two lines for the new chord. This is all done for a good reason. With our new chords we only have two sets for each key. Like in the key of C major, one set of chords starts at the third position and the other set at the 8th position. This helps you in many ways. One is that we eliminate all of those unnecessary chords that there are for guitar. Another great help is that once you mastered both sets for each key, you will be able to transpose from one key to another with great ease.

Getting back to the chords, you may notice that most of the time when we have a seventh chord, we substitute minor chords in their place. If the chord is G7, I may use Dmi7 to Dmi6, or Dmi7 to G13, or something like that. The fifth of any dominant chord can be substituted in place of the Dominant itself. Let's say that you have two bars of D7, All right, the 5th of D is A, All you have to do is count up with your fingers D, E, F, G, then A. A-minor is a very close relative to D7. Now you know that if you have a dominant 7 chord you can substitute its relative minor which is the 5th of the chord.

In order to really get an understanding of this, you must write out all dominant 7 chords from C7 up to B7 and beside them put the relative minor like this: — the 5th of C7 is G minor, the 5th of D♭7 is B♭ minor, and go always up to B7 and F♯ minor. After you have done this I want you to make chord charts similar to that of Lesson No. 11 in the keys of D♭, E♭, F, G, A♭ and B♭. By doing this you will get all of your most important chords on charts for each key to refer to.

I think that the best thing for you to do is to make up a scrap book, and put all of this material in it for reference at all times. Now, if you can't understand all of what I'm trying to tell you right away, don't worry too much about it. But if you keep reviewing each lesson that you don't quite understand it will all come to you as you keep studying.

Just remember that every lesson is important, and should be studied over and over again.

LESSON 13

Now we come to vamps. Vamps are very important in jump tunes and novelty tunes.

There are many ways to play these vamps, but I'm only writing out the most important progressions for now.

After you have worked these vamps out in this key which is C major, transpose them to the keys of: D♭, E♭, F, G, A♭, and B♭, then make up charts similar to this one in each key. Then practice them in every key.

Try playing these vamps string bass style (see Lesson No. 8) and arpeggio style. This will make the vamp sound fuller and better.

Standard

C Gdim | Dmi G7 | C Gdim | Dmi G7 | C C7 | F Fmi | C Gdim | Dmi G7

New

(16) Cma7 (4) Ami7 | (18) Dmi7 (23) G13 | (16) Cma7 (4) Ami7 | (18) Dmi7 (23) G13 | (16) Cma7 (6) C13 ♭5♭9 | (2) Fma7 (4) Fmi7 | (16) Cma7 (18) E♭mi7 | Dmi7 (21) G7 ♯5♭9

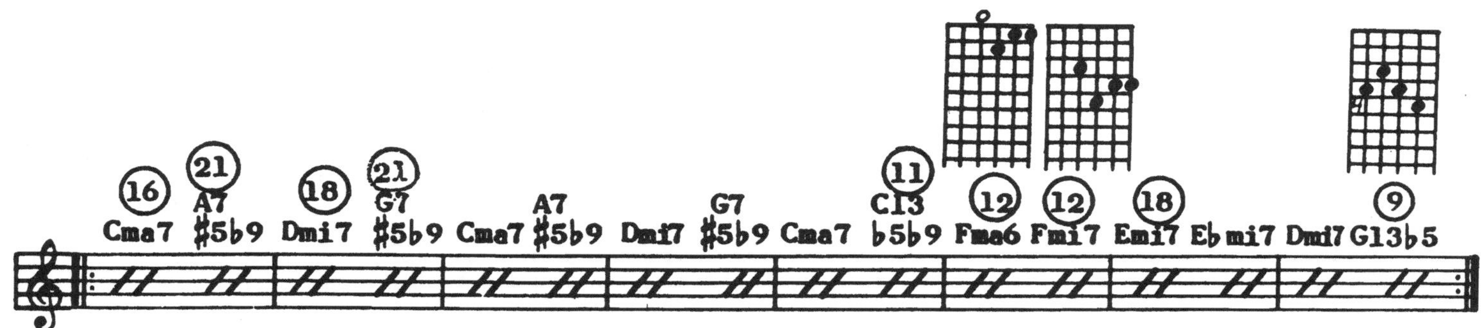

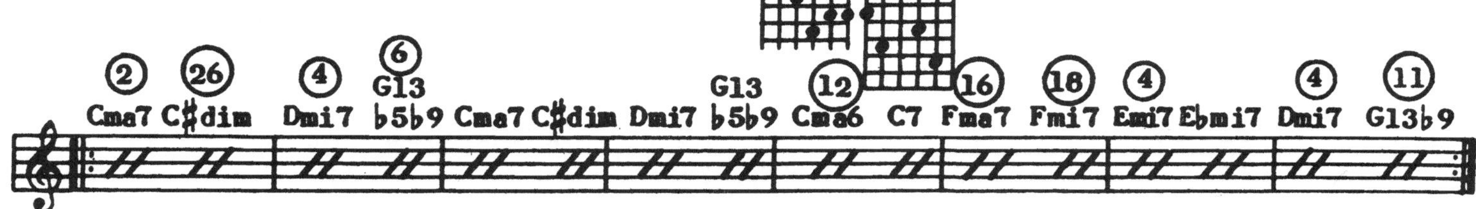

LESSON 14

Here are a few more nice vamp ideas for fill-ins when you play behind horn players. We have to change our key for this to get the best results.

This can't be done so easily in the key of C major. so we move up to the key of G major

In order to work out these vamps, I will have to introduce a few new chords We will call them chords No. 27, 28. 29 and 30.

After you have learned these vamps in Key of G major take each one separately and transpose it to as many keys as you possibly can. They will have to be done separately, because you can't play them all in every key.

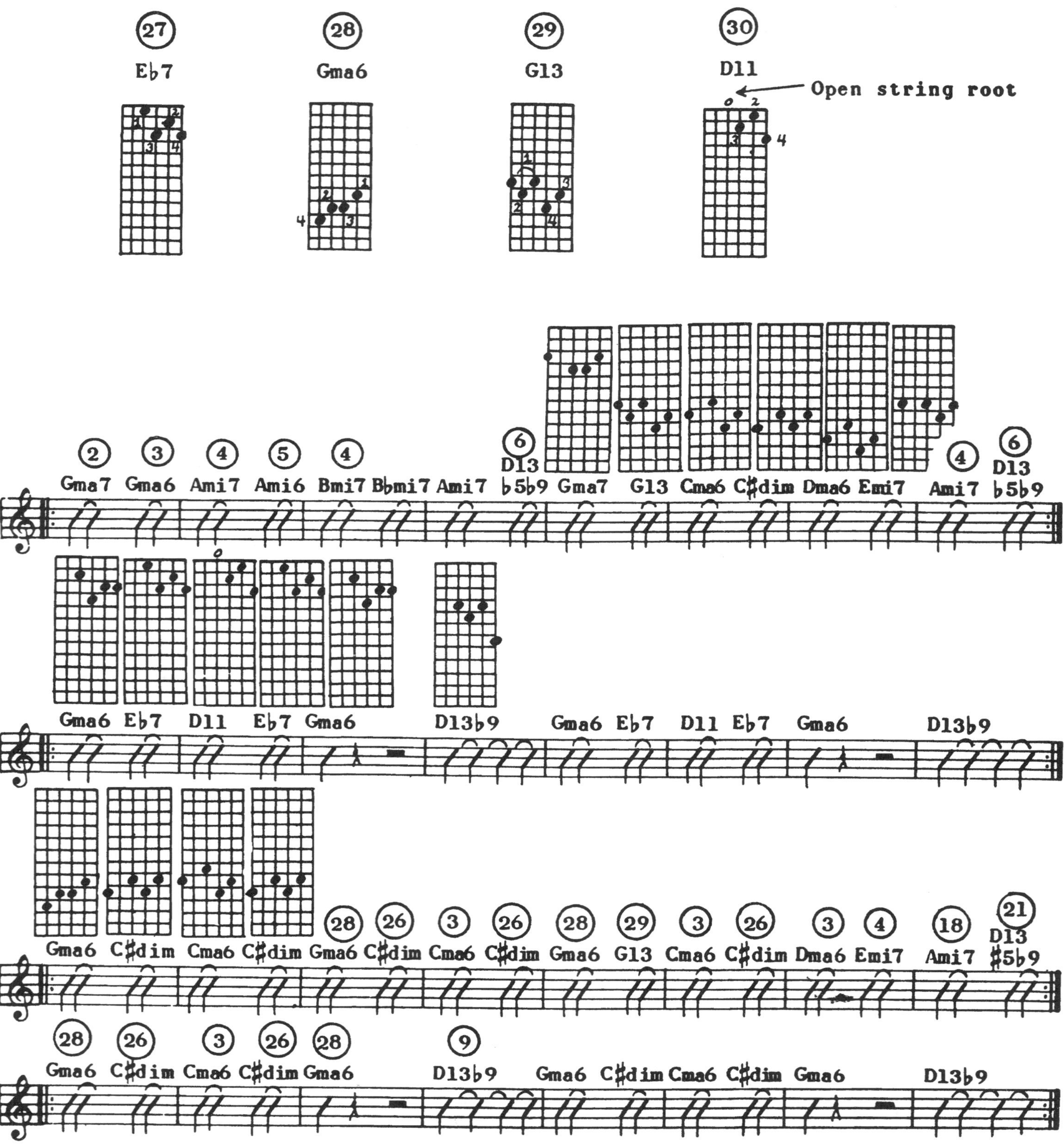

LESSON 15

Now we will work with bridges.

In this Lesson I have written out three of the most used bridges in Jazz. They are written as always, standard chords at the top, and new chords at the bottom of each example.

These bridges are for the key of C major. After you have worked them out, transpose them to the keys of: D♭, E♭, F, G, A♭ and B♭. Then make up charts in each key.

If you should come across a few chord progressions that are very hard to play, work on them continually until you can play them comfortably.

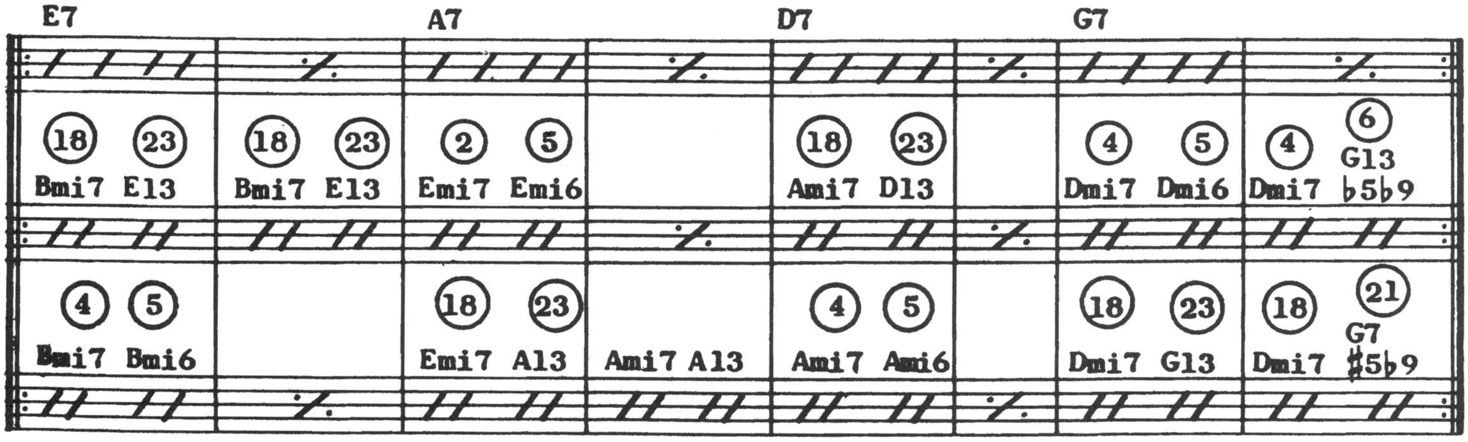

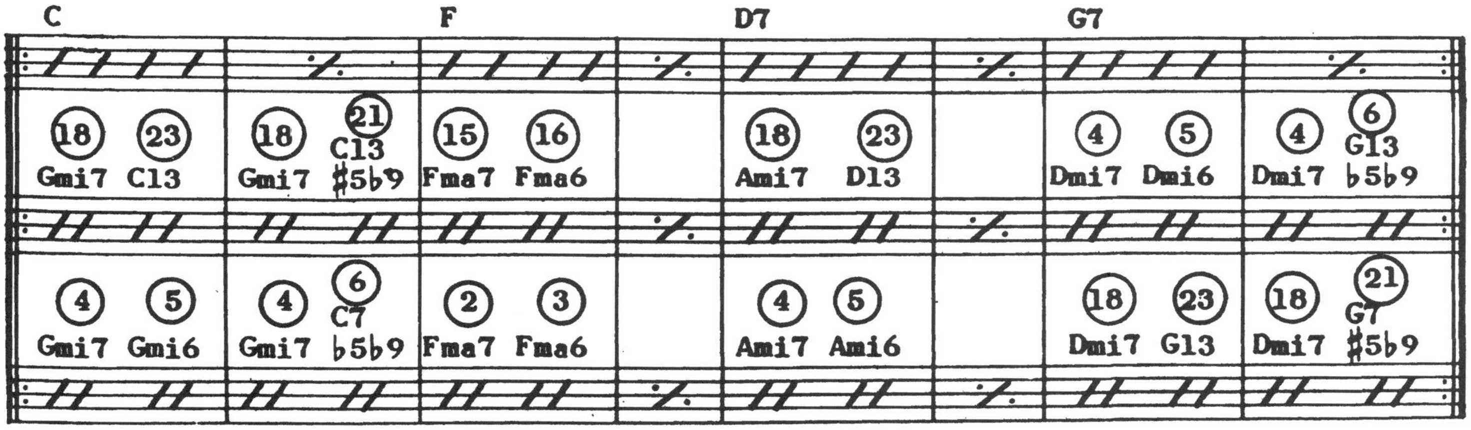

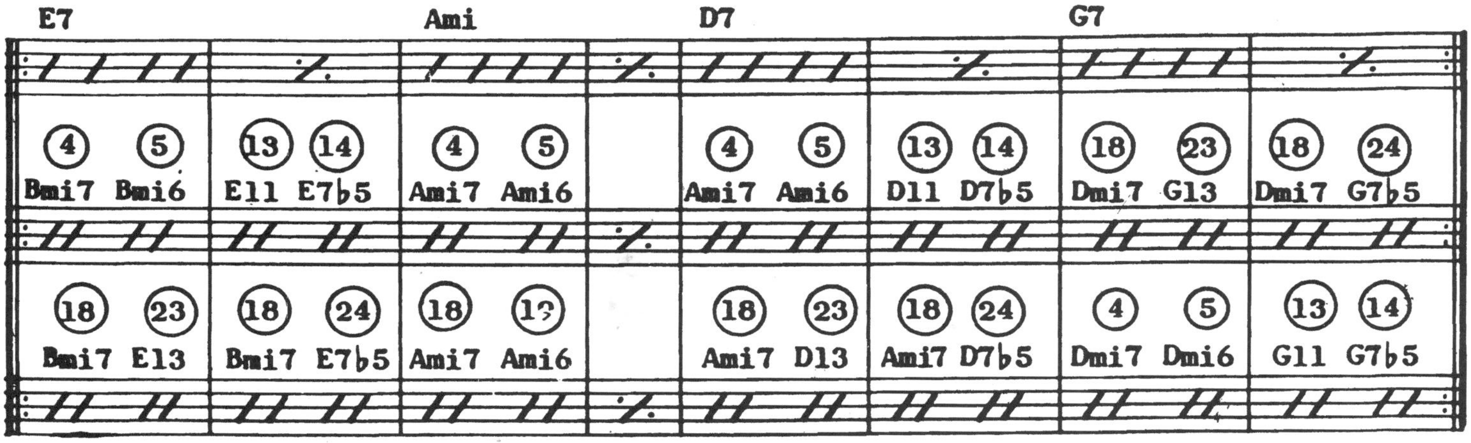

E7		A7		D7		G7	
(18) (23) Bmi7 E13	(18) (23) Bmi7 E13	(2) (5) Emi7 Emi6		(18) (23) Ami7 D13		(4) (5) Dmi7 Dmi6	(4) (6) Dmi7 G13 ♭5♭9
(4) (5) Bmi7 Bmi6		(18) (23) Emi7 A13	Ami7 A13	(4) (5) Ami7 Ami6		(18) (23) Dmi7 G13	(18) (21) Dmi7 G7 ♯5♭9

C		F		D7		G7	
(18) (23) Gmi7 C13	(18) (21) Gmi7 C13 ♯5♭9	(15) (16) Fma7 Fma6		(18) (23) Ami7 D13		(4) (5) Dmi7 Dmi6	(4) (6) Dmi7 G13 ♭5♭9
(4) (5) Gmi7 Gmi6	(4) (6) Gmi7 C7 ♭5♭9	(2) (3) Fma7 Fma6		(4) (5) Ami7 Ami6		(18) (23) Dmi7 G13	(18) (21) Dmi7 G7 ♯5♭9

E7		Ami		D7		G7	
(4) (5) Bmi7 Bmi6	(13) (14) E11 E7♭5	(4) (5) Ami7 Ami6		(4) (5) Ami7 Ami6	(13) (14) D11 D7♭5	(18) (23) Dmi7 G13	(18) (24) Dmi7 G7♭5
(18) (23) Bmi7 E13	(18) (24) Bmi7 E7♭5	(18) (13) Ami7 Ami6		(18) (23) Ami7 D13	(18) (24) Ami7 D7♭5	(4) (5) Dmi7 Dmi6	(13) (14) G11 G7♭5

LESSON 16

Now for the last lesson in chord progressions.

If you are still a little shaky on your chords, and feel that you don't know them too well up to this point, review these lessons two or three times a week, and you will find that everything will come to you as you keep studying.

This Lesson is the key to all of the other lessons. Here I have written out the best possible way to connect one chord to another using the dominant as leading chord for each example.

First, we have dominant to dominant connections, second, we have dominant to minor connections; and third, dominant to major connections. With these few chord connections you can build progressions around any song. All you have to do is keep working with them until you find the one that fits best. As you work with these chords you will begin to develop an ear for them. Then as soon as you hear a song you will know just what chord connections to use.

After you have worked each of these examples out, make up charts similar to this one in the keys of: D♭, E♭, F, G, A♭ and B♭ (See lesson No. 12)

Standard

G7	C7	G7	Cmi	G7	Cma
New (18) Dmi7 (23) G13	(4) Gmi7 (5) Gmi6	(18) Dmi7 (23) G13	(18) Cmi7 (19) Cmi6	(18) Dmi7 (23) G13	(16) Cma7 (17) Cma6
(18) Dmi7 (24) G7♭5	(13) C11 (14) C7♭5	(18) Dmi7 (24) G7♭5	Cmi7 Cmi6	(18) Dmi7 (24) G7♭5	Cma7 Cma6
(23) G13	(5) Gmi6	(18) Dmi7 (21) G7♯5♭9	Cmi7 Cmi6	(18) Dmi7 (21) G7♯5♭9	Cma7 Cma6
(4) Dmi7 (5) Dmi6	(18) Gmi7 (23) C13	(4) Dmi7 (5) Dmi6	(4) Cmi7 (5) Cmi6	(4) Dmi7 (5) Dmi6	(2) Cma7 (3) Cma6
(13) G11 (14) G7♭5	(18) Cmi7 (24) C7♭5	(4) Dmi7 (26) Ddim	Cmi7 Cmi6	(4) Dmi7 (6) G13♭5♭9	Cma7 Cma6
(5) Dmi6	(23) C13	(13) G11 (14) G7♭5	Cmi7 Cmi6	(13) G11 (14) G7♭5	Cma7 Cma6

LESSON 17

Now we are at the point where you are to put your knowledge of chords to work. Up until now you have studied how to use chords. Now I want you to use them.

Get four or five sheet music's (popular tunes) or any kind of songs that you like. Study the chord connections, then take your new chords and apply them to these songs. You may not be so successful at first, but keep working with your chord charts, and using every trick you can think of until you get it.

Every day you should take a couple of songs, and make up chord patterns for them until it becomes natural

LESSON 18

In your next few lessons I have written introductions, endings, and a lot of chord tricks that modern guitarists use. After you learn all of the material, you should put it to work right away. This material can be used with most any melody, so what you should do first, is to listen to the melody of a song, then try different introductions on them, do the same with endings.

With these chords there are a world of things that can be done. A lot can be done toward developing your ear by constantly listening to songs and working out progressions for them.

So keep reviewing these lessons, and try to make up new ideas from those that you have. Another thing is to get standard chord books, which carry the chords to all of the old tunes. They will be very helpful to you in working out chord progressions. You can get them at your local music store.

You are also to transpose each introduction to as many keys as possible, and the same with the endings, and the other material.

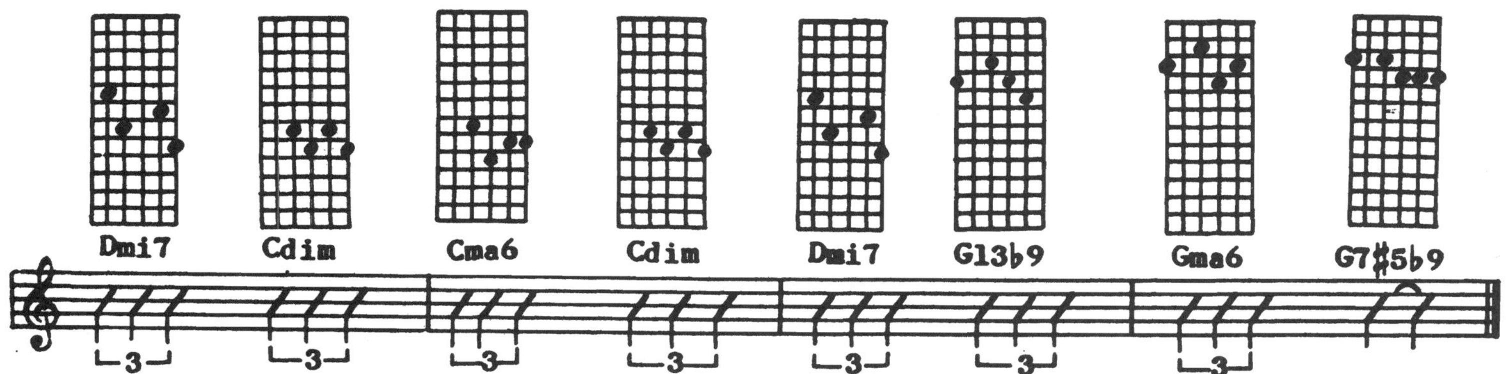

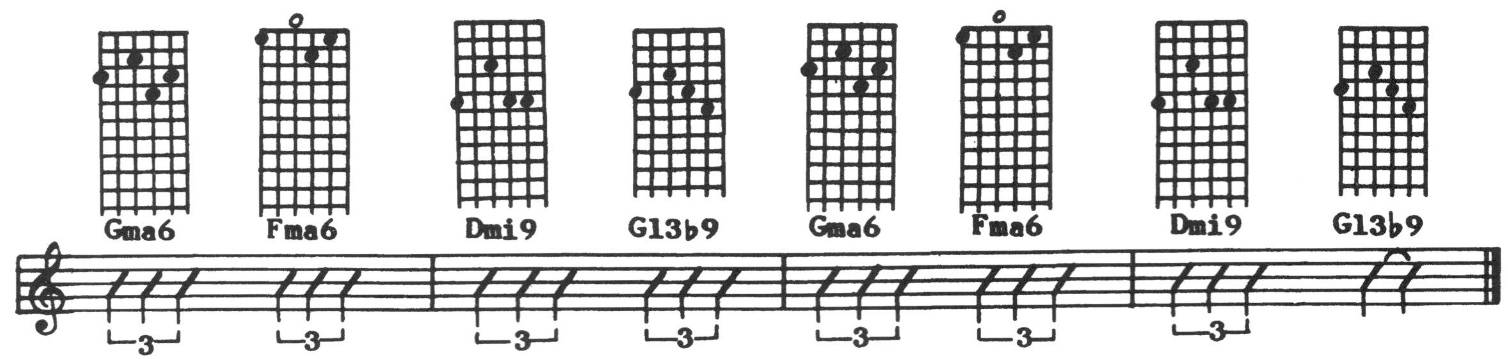
Gma6
Fma6
Dmi9
G13♭9
Gma6
Fma6
Dmi9
G13♭9
3
3
3
3
3
3
3

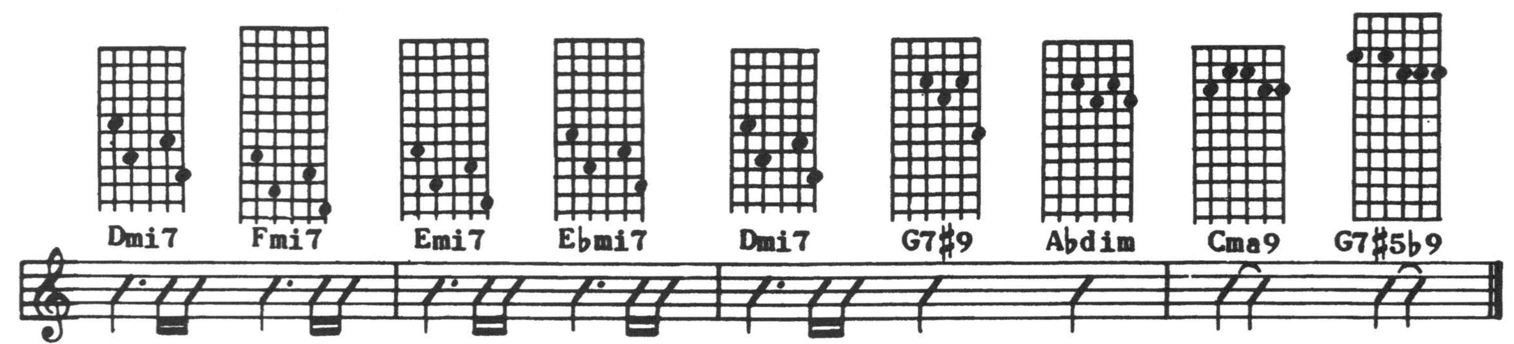
Dmi7
Fmi7
Emi7
E♭mi7
Dmi7
G7♯9
A♭dim
Cma9
G7♯5♭9

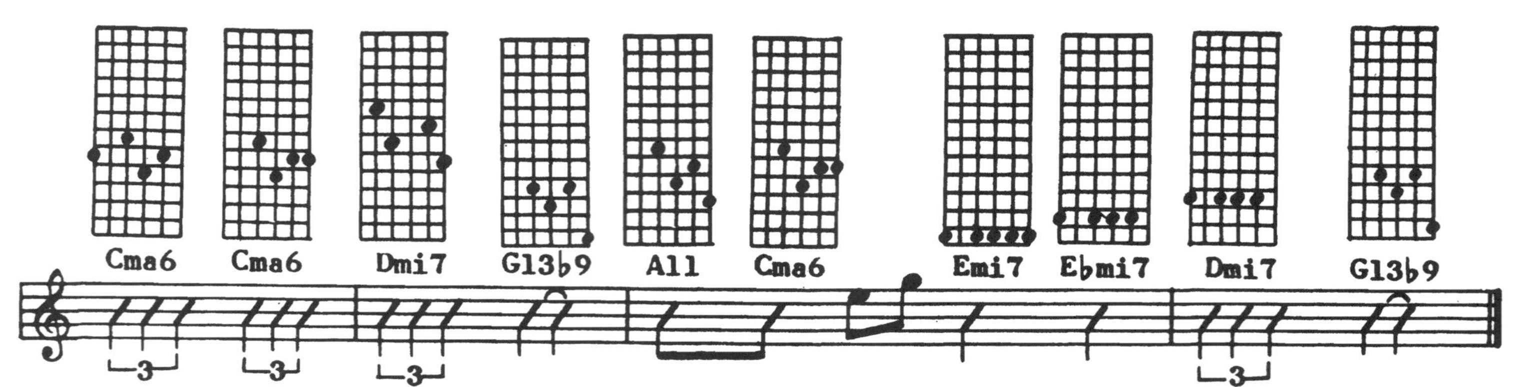
Cma6
Cma6
Dmi7
G13♭9
All
Cma6
Emi7
E♭mi7
Dmi7
G13♭9
3
3
3
3

LESSON 19

In this lesson we are going back to harmony just a little bit, and I will try to explain about chords with two names. Also I am introducing a few more chords.

When we are in one key a chord may be Gma♭ while still in another key — the same chord has a different name, Emi7. Below I have analyzed the harmonic structure of these chords. You are to learn both names of these chords in all keys.

Its best to write them out in your work book like this, Gma6 is also Emi7; A♭ma6 is also Fmi7. Do this chromatically always up the finger board with each chord, because in the next few lessons I'm using these chords, and both names in some progressions. A lot of these progressions will not be diagrammed as they were before. I'll simply write the chord and put its number over it, so it will be up to you to find them.

NEW CHORDS

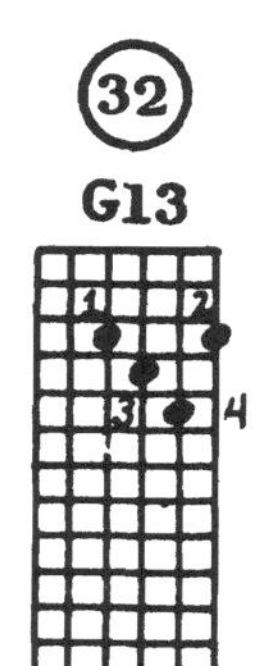

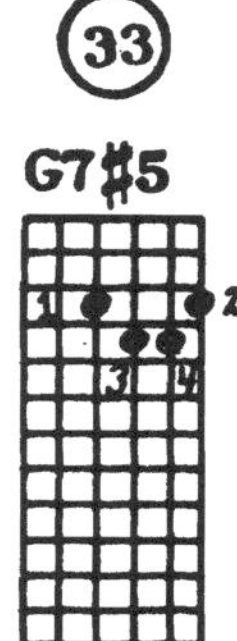

BELOW WE HAVE AN ANALYSIS OF CHORDS WITH TWO NAMES

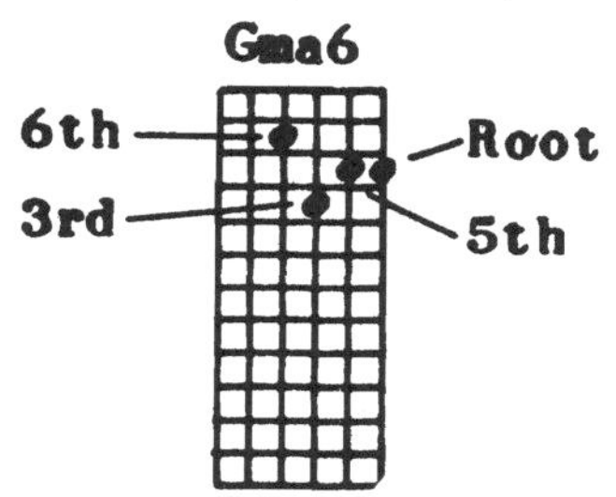

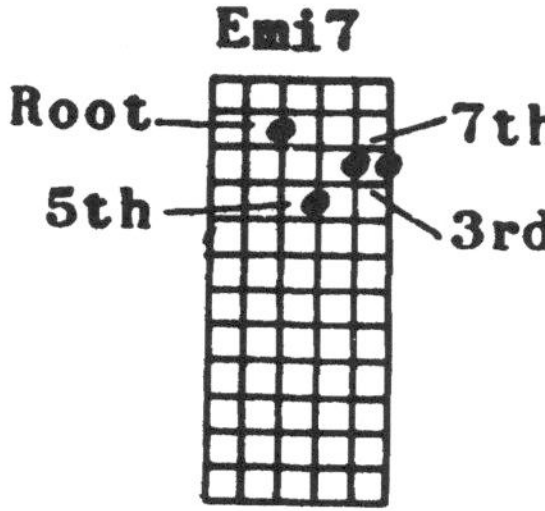

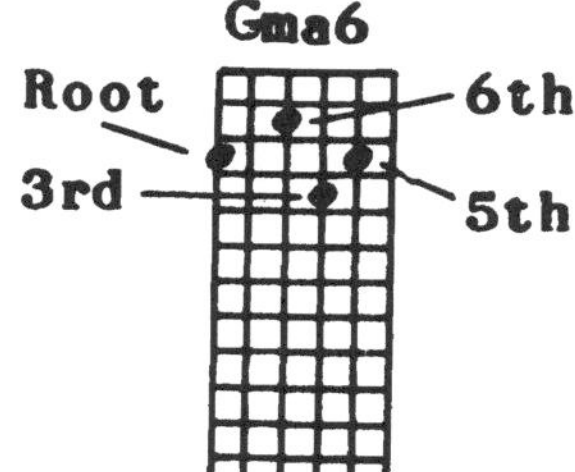

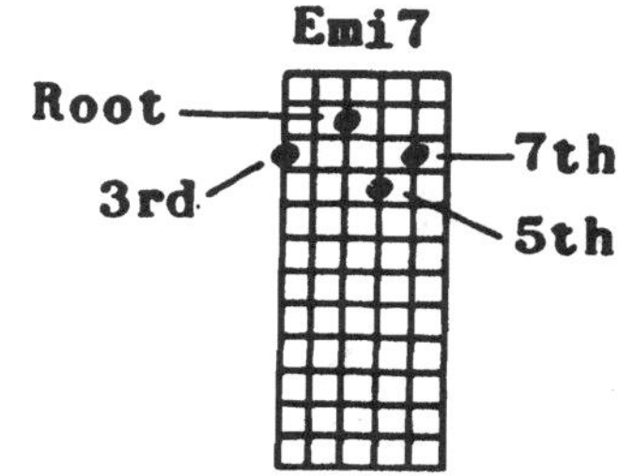

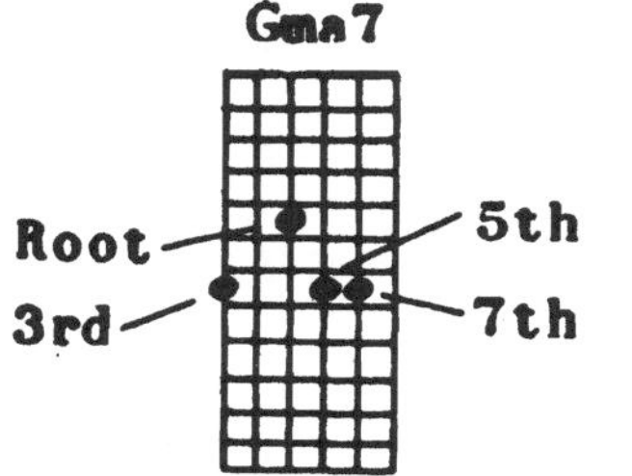

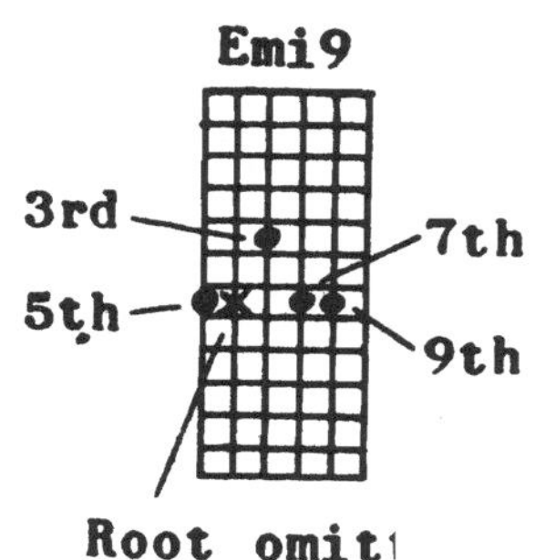

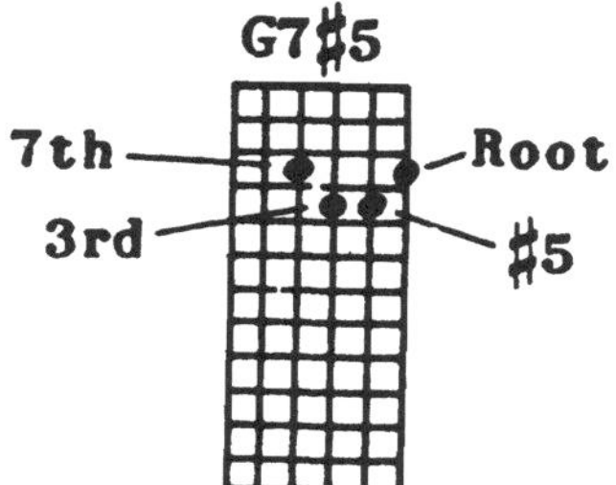

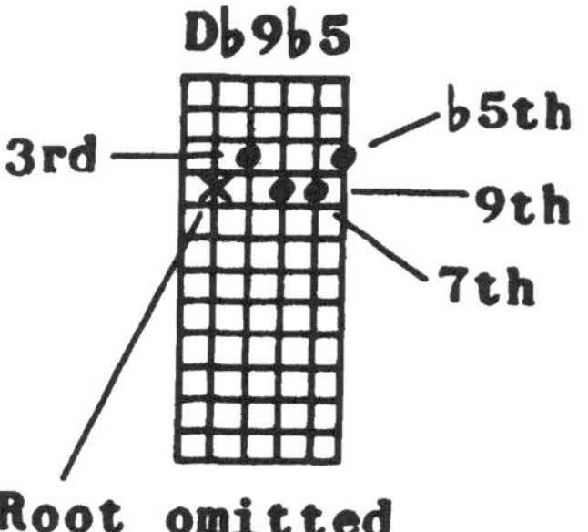

LESSON 20
(Intro's In G Major)

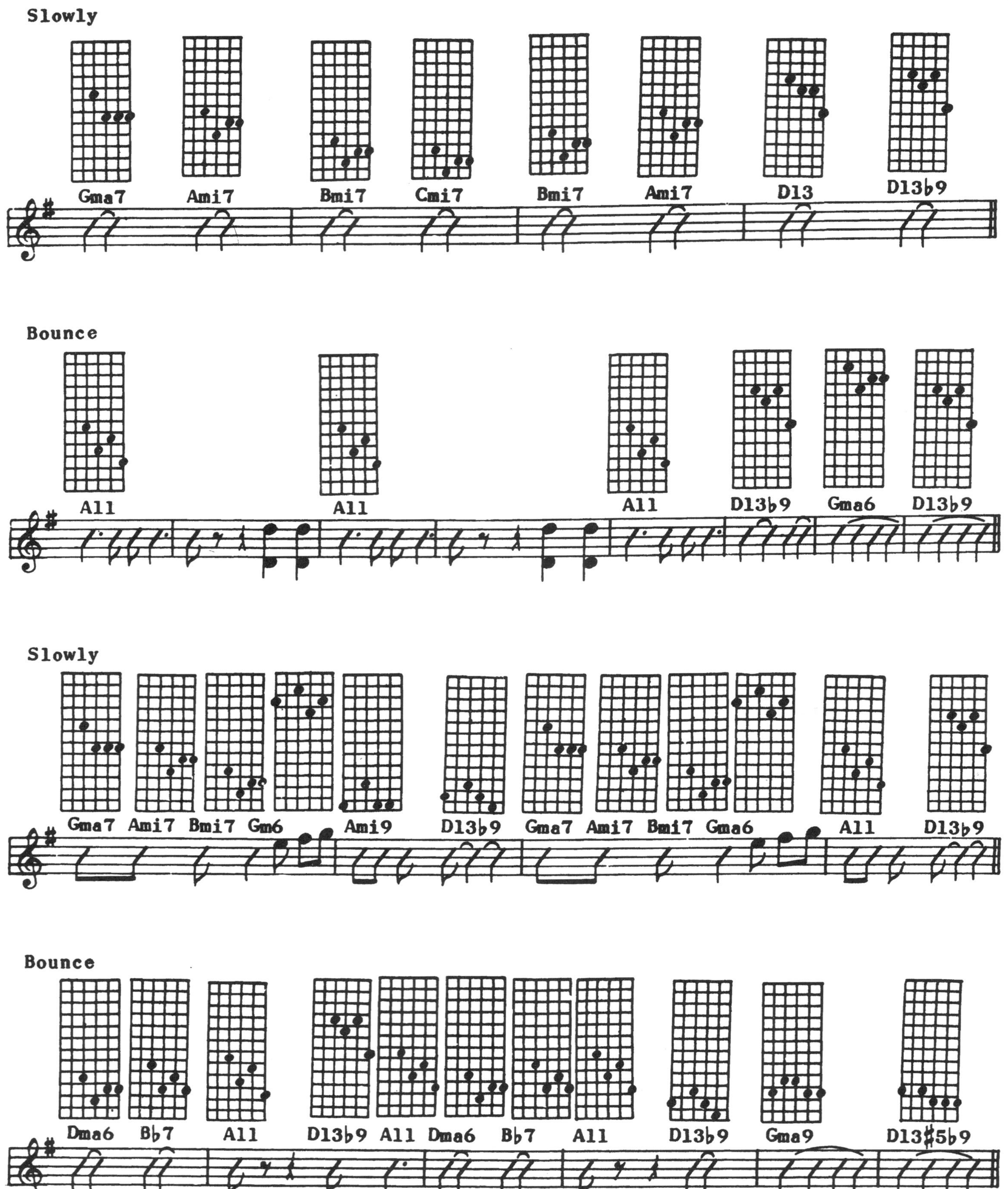

LESSON 21
BOP BLUES PROGRESSIONS IN G MAJOR

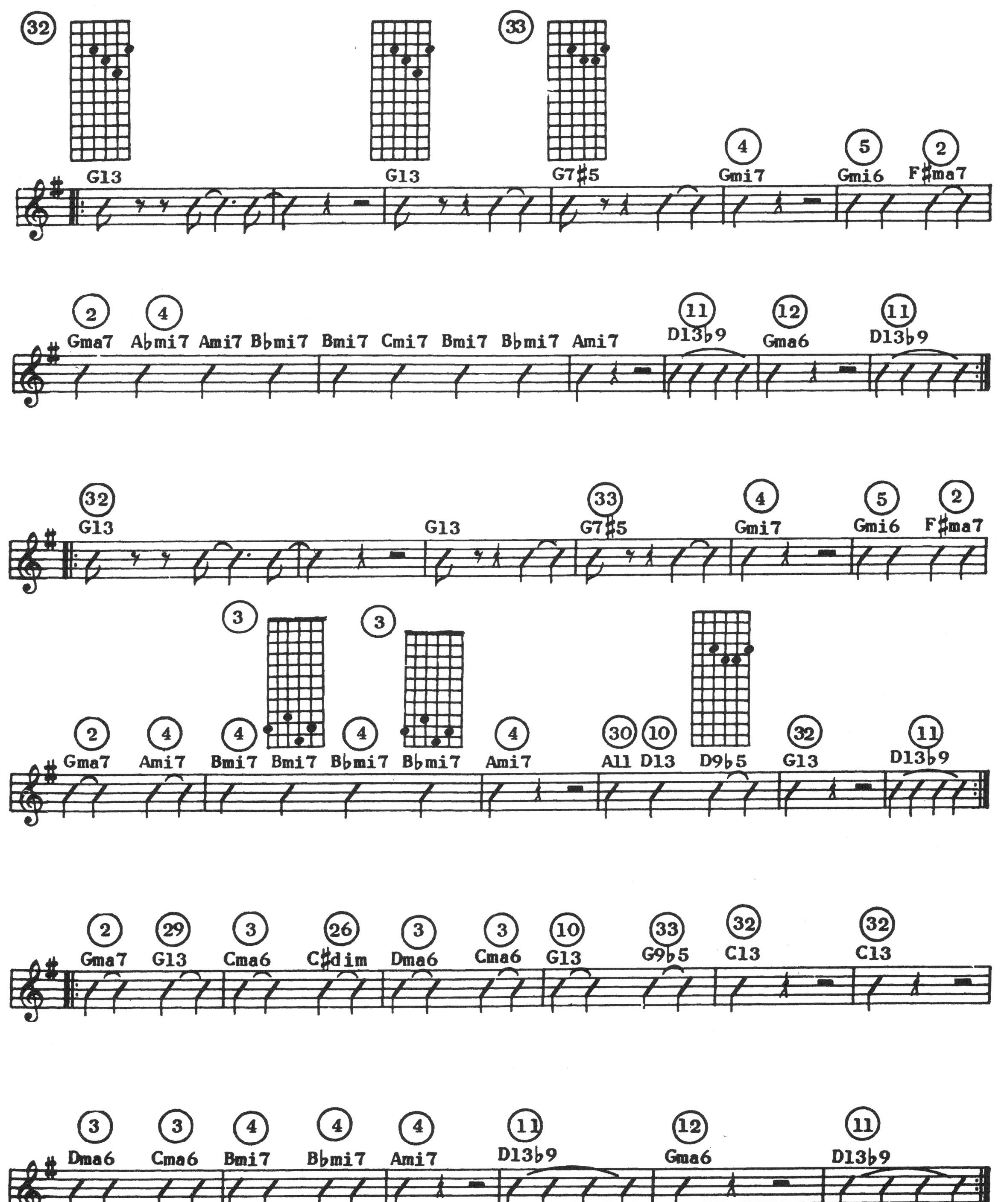

LESSON 22
ENDINGS IN G MAJOR

*S. is to indicate the string the note is on.
F. is to indicate the fingering.

LESSON 23

In this, our last lesson in chord study, I have written out some of the most used chord progressions in Jazz today. These are standard changes, and if you analyze them and work with them long enough, you will find that they appear in many different songs in various places.

There are eleven different examples and below each example I have the new changes that sound best in their places. Work them out thoroughly in the keys that they are in, then make up charts of each in all of the other keys: — F, G, A♭, B♭, C, D♭, and E♭. Then work them out in these new keys.

These charts will be very helpful to you in transposing from one key to another. They will also play a very important part in Lesson No. 35 and 46 (See Lesson No. 45 and 46).

8 BAR SEQUENCES
(Chord Cycles)

No. 1

Standard:

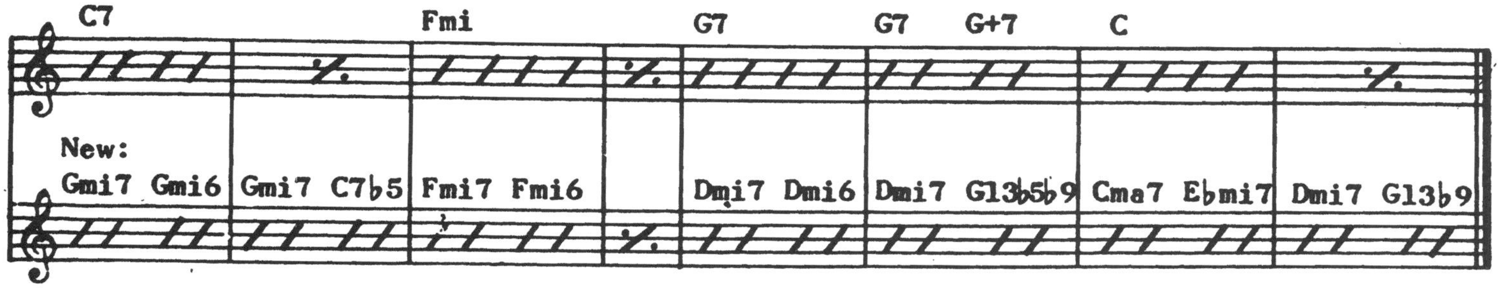

C7 | % | Fmi | % | G7 | G7 G+7 | C | %

New:

Gmi7 Gmi6 | Gmi7 C7♭5 | Fmi7 Fmi6 | % | Dmi7 Dmi6 | Dmi7 G13♭5♭9 | Cma7 E♭mi7 | Dmi7 G13♭9

No. 2

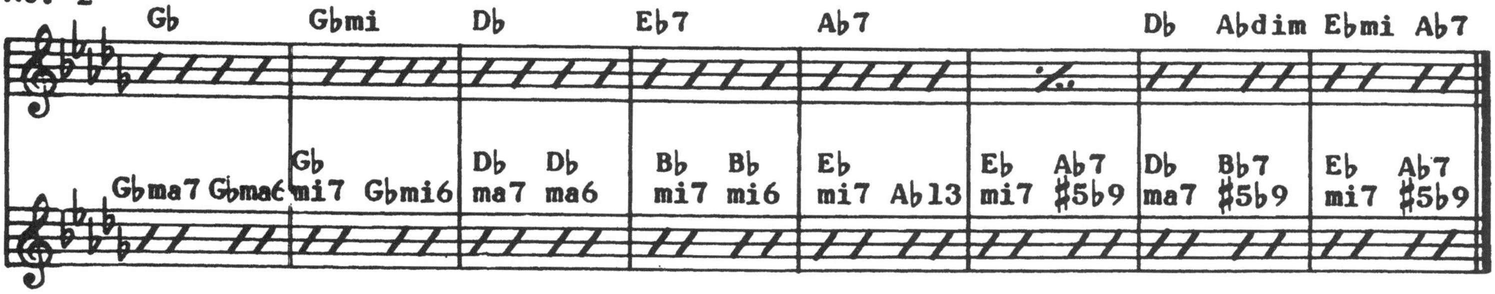

G♭ | G♭mi | D♭ | E♭7 | A♭7 | % | D♭ A♭dim | E♭mi A♭7

G♭ma7 G♭ma6 | G♭ mi7 G♭mi6 | D♭ ma7 D♭ ma6 | B♭ mi7 B♭ mi6 | E♭ mi7 A♭13 | E♭ mi7 A♭7 ♯5♭9 | D♭ ma7 B♭7 ♯5♭9 | E♭ mi7 A♭7 ♯5♭9

No. 3

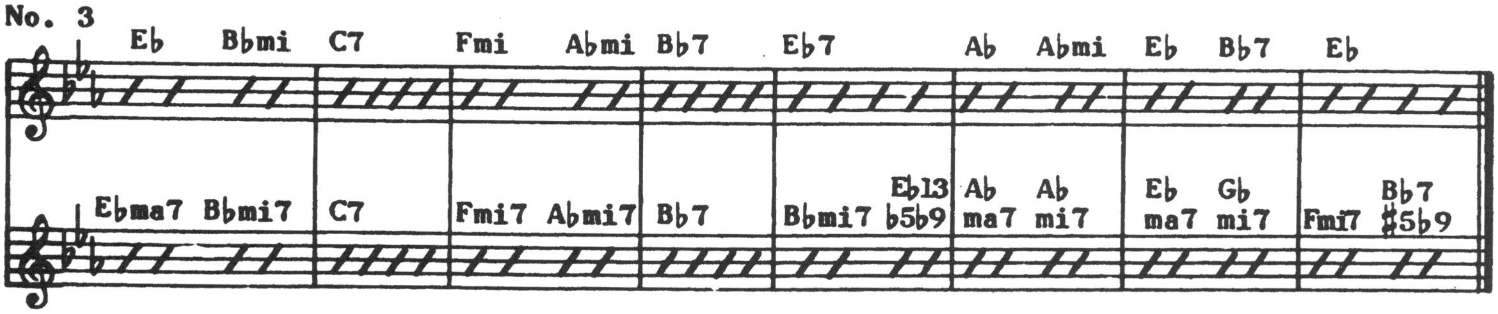

E♭ B♭mi | C7 | Fmi A♭mi | B♭7 | E♭7 | A♭ A♭mi | E♭ B♭7 | E♭

E♭ma7 B♭mi7 | C7 | Fmi7 A♭mi7 | B♭7 | B♭mi7 E♭13 ♭5♭9 | A♭ ma7 A♭ mi7 | E♭ ma7 G♭ mi7 | Fmi7 B♭7 ♯5♭9

16 BAR SEQUENCES
(Chord Cycles)

No. 8
Standard:
G
E♭7
G
E7
Ami
E7
Ami
E♭7
D7

New:
Gma7 Gma6
B♭mi7 B♭mi6
Gma7 Gma6
Bmi7 Bmi6
E11 E7♭5
Ami7 Ami6
E11 E7♭5
Ami7 Ami6
B♭mi7 B♭mi6
Ami7 Ami6
Ami7 D13♭5♭9

No. 9

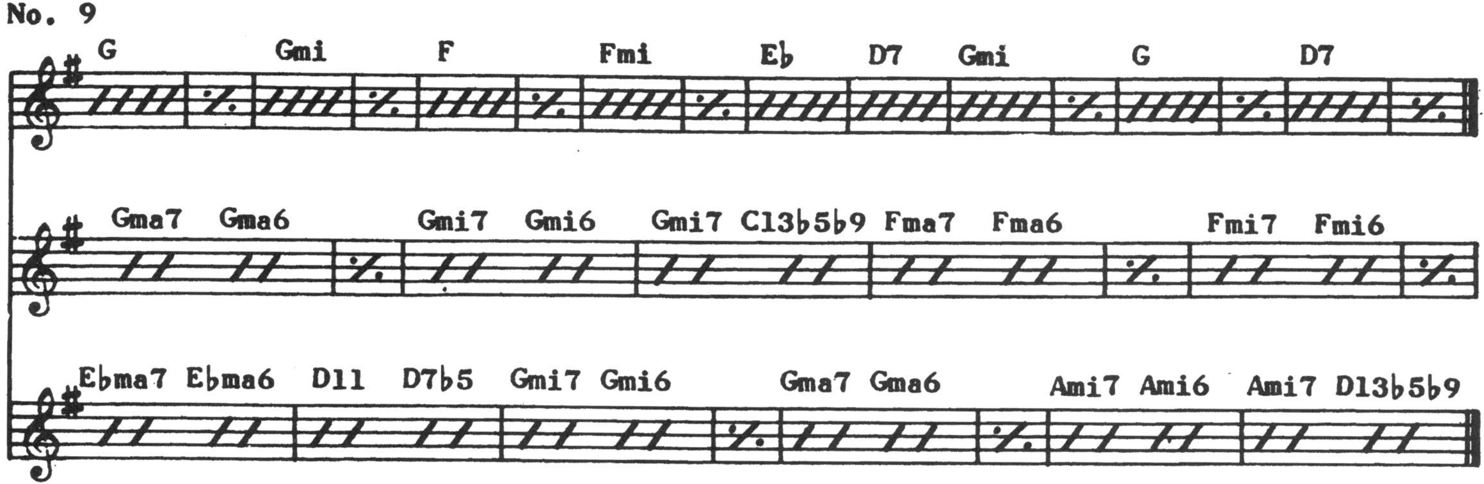

No. 10

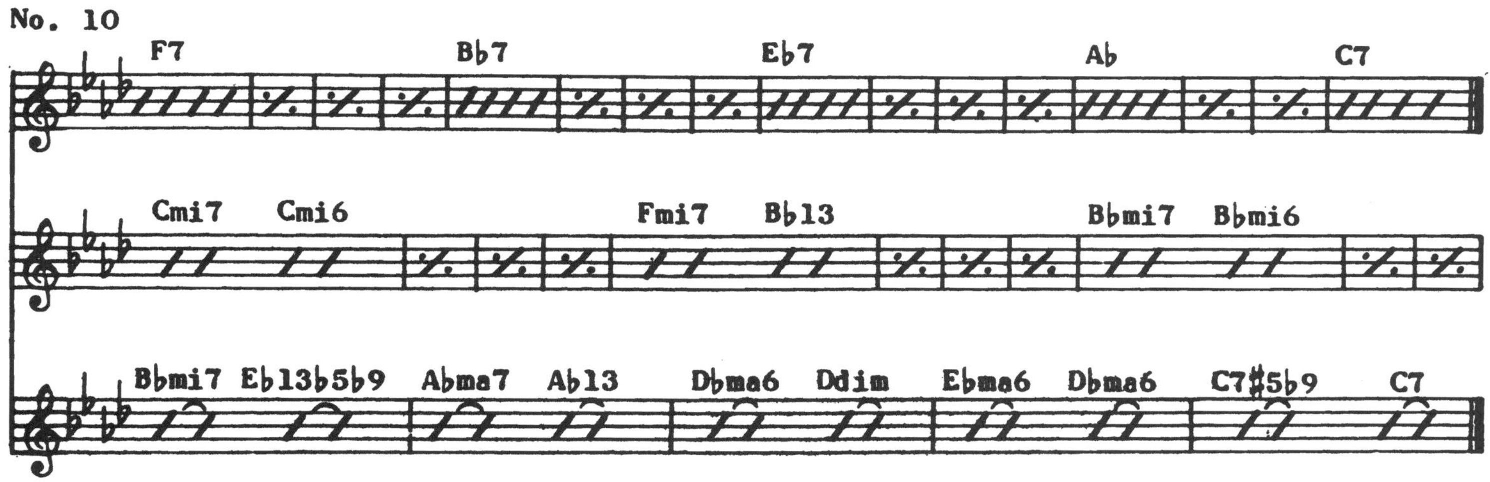

No. 11

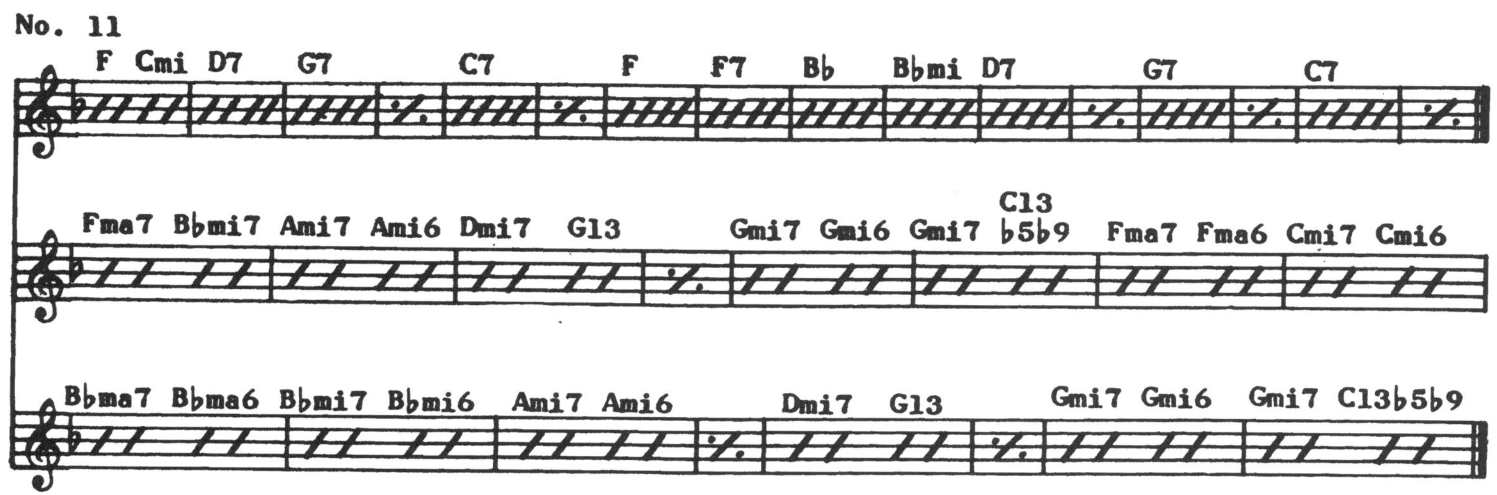

PART TWO

Now that you know how to use chords, let's go into the most important study which is solo work. This is where guitarists have the most trouble. Solo work is really very simple if you know how to do it. Of course, I know it seems impossible to stand up and take a solo if you're not familiar with the rudiments of the idea.

But before we go into this I want to make a few points clear to you, and you should always keep this in mind. It is impossible for anyone to teach you how to feel music, that is, to stand up and play solos one after another. This has to come from your soul. Now, in order to develop a soul for music, these are the things you must do constantly. Practice playing your guitar with records, listen to solos by horn players, learn to steal solos from records. Anything that you hear another musician play, try to play it yourself. Strum the chords to any song that you like and hum ideas, — then apply the ideas to the guitar. This will be hard to do at first and some of it may sound silly, but if you keep doing this long enough you will develop an ear for music, and once you have an ear you'll be stealing solos from everybody and building your own ideas around them. You will also develop a beautiful soul for music which will in time enable you to play anything you want to at will.

Another very important thing for you to do is to hang around jam sessions. Do as much sitting with other musicians as possible. Doing this will help to develop an ear for music and it also helps with your timing. If you know another guitarist get together with him as much as possible, — let him strum chords for you while you take solos, and you do likewise for him.

In PART TWO of this book I have set down all the material that is necessary to make you a solo guitarist. So, follow my instructions to the letter, and remember everything that I have told you.

Also, give each Lesson at least two hours study a day!

LESSON 24

I know that you are eager to run right through this material, but remember, if you rush these lessons you won't know any more when you finish the book than you did when you started. So let's just take our time and do each lesson as I tell you to.

First, we have exercises from Lesson 24 to 30. Each one is as important to you as eating and sleeping, because within these 28 exercises lies the key to solo work. So you are to live with them for the rest of your life. I know you can't learn them within the few weeks that I have them set in. It took years for me myself to master them. So every time you pick up your instrument you should go over each exercise.

Remember, don't rush! Go into this section of the book very slowly. Take each exercise and practice it as slowly as possible. Only increase the tempo when you can play it relaxed at a slow tempo. Remember, if you cannot play an exercise slowly, you surely can't play it fast.

Every exercise and solo in this book is to be played with an up and down stroke. In order to play with an up and down stroke you must start right now to using nothing other. Anything that you play from now on, you are to use up and down strokes.

You are to learn the name of these exercises by heart from one end of the guitar to the other. This will not only make you more familiar with your instrument, but each of these runs will play a very important part in your solo work.

TIME VALUES AND EXERCISES
(In The Key Of C, 1st Position)

The sign "X" is for open string.
The sign "S" is for the string.
The sign "F" is for the fingering.

Ex. 1

LESSON 25
WRIST DEVELOPMENT
(With Up And Down Strokes)

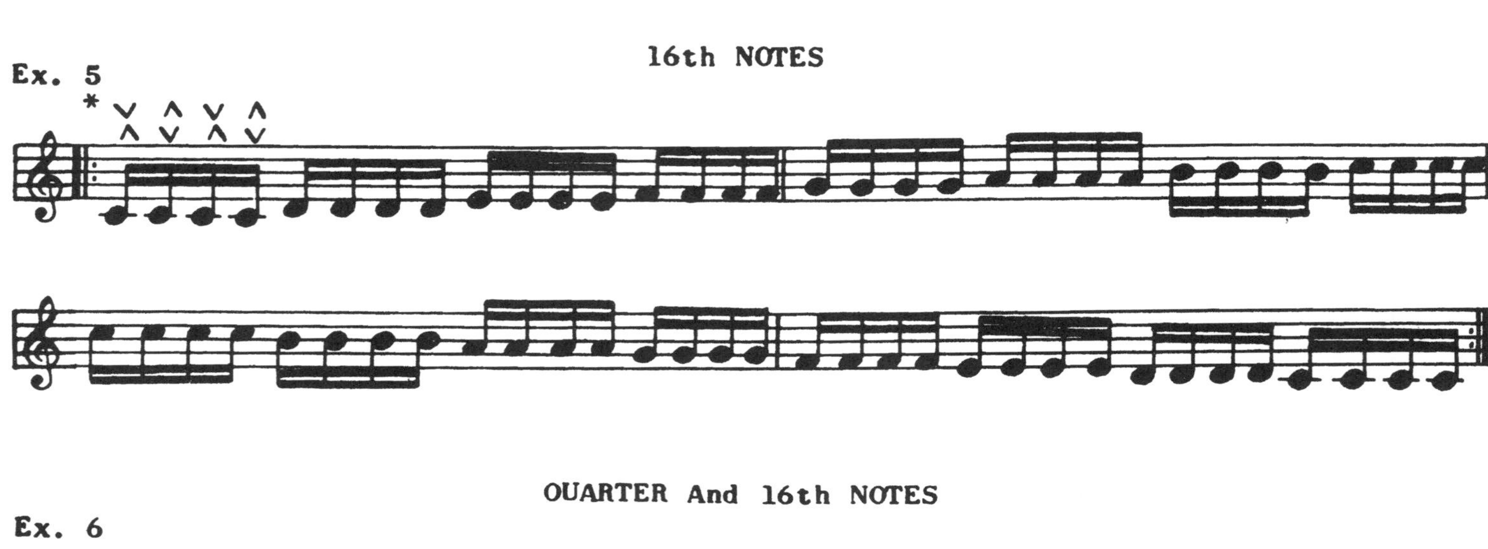

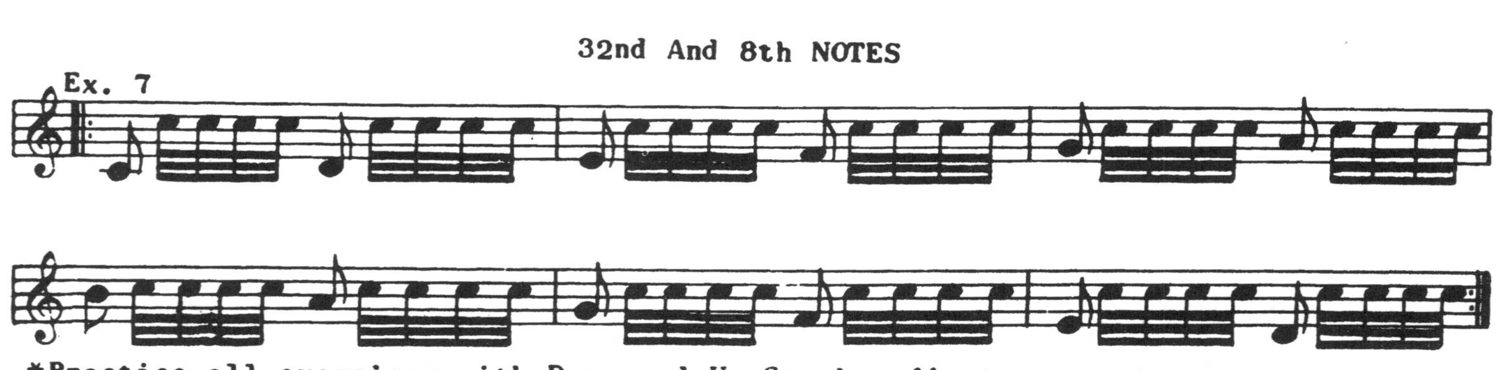

*Practice all exercises with Down and Up Strokes first. ∧∨∧∨∧∨.
Then with up and down. ∨∧∨∧∨∧∨.

LESSON 26
SCALES AND EXERCISES
(In The Key Of A Minor)

HARMONIC MINOR

Ex. 8

MELODIC MINOR

Ex. 9

MORE WRIST DEVELOPMENT

Ex. 10

Ex. 11

FASTER

Ex. 12

LESSON 27
SCALE RUNS
(In F Position)

SCALE RUNS
(In D♭ Position)

LESSON 28
MINOR 7th RUNS

Practice chromatically (As in Lesson 27)

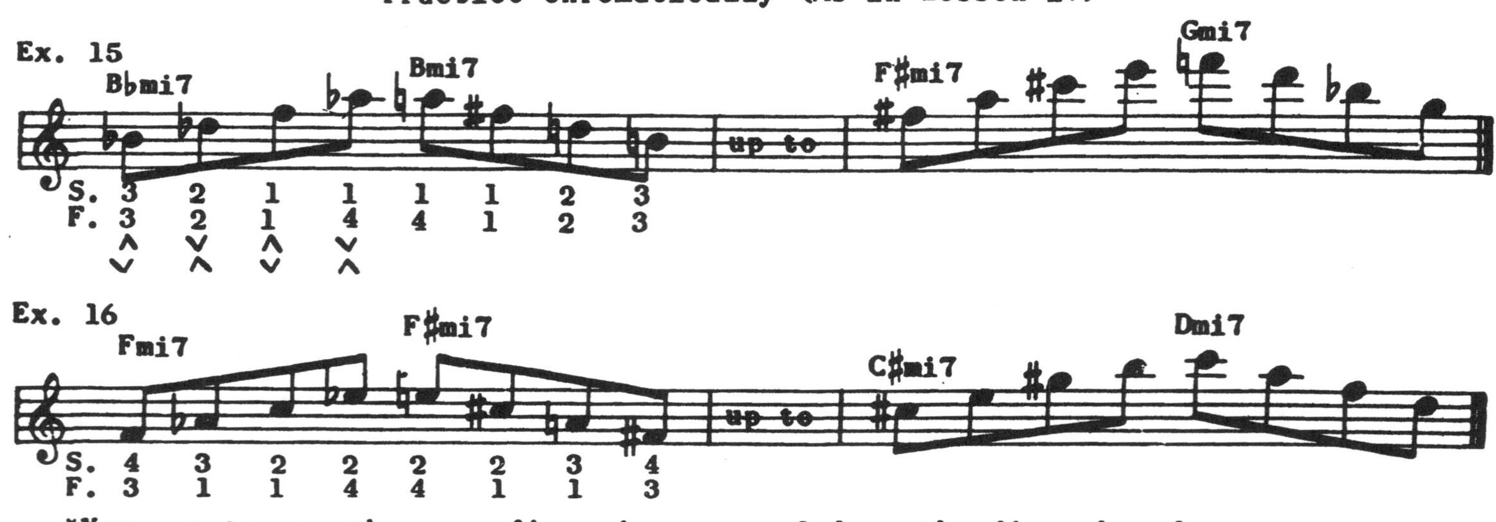

*You are to use the same fingering, up and down the fingerboard.

Ex. 17

E♭mi7
Emi7
up to
Bmi7
Cmi7

S.	4	4	3	2	2	3	4	4
F.	1	4	3	2	2	3	4	1

Ex. 18

B♭mi7
Bmi7
up to
F♯mi7
Gmi7

S.	5	5	4	3	3	4	5	5
F.	1	4	3	1	1	3	4	1

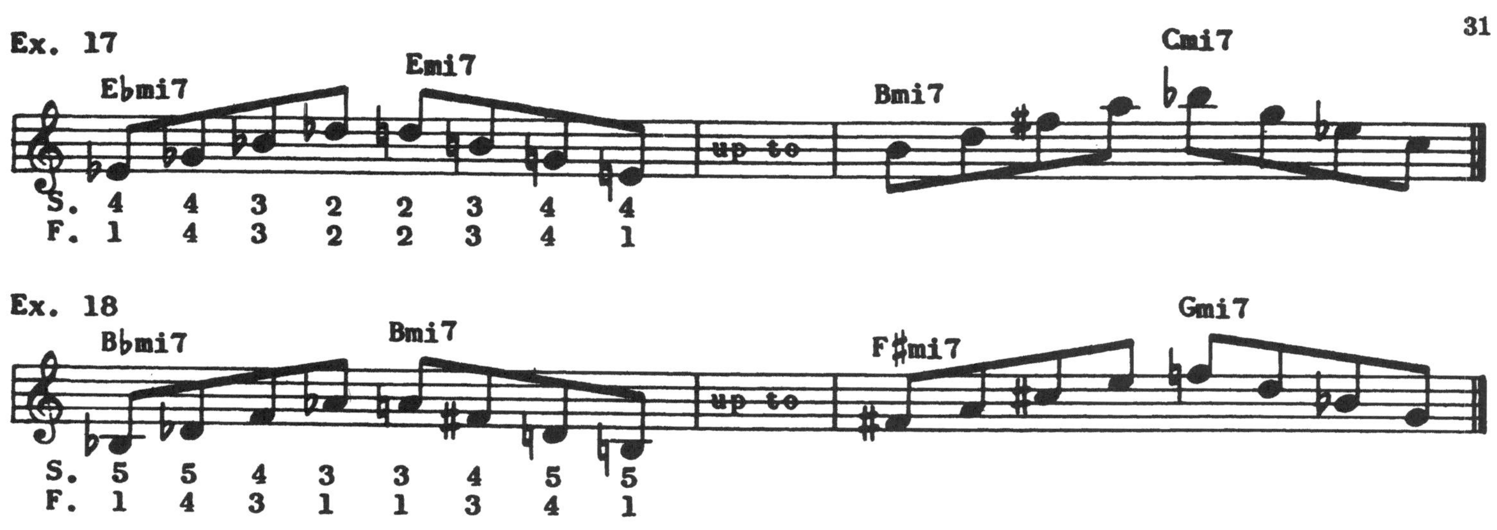

LESSON 29
DOMINANT 7th AND 9th RUNS

Ex. 19

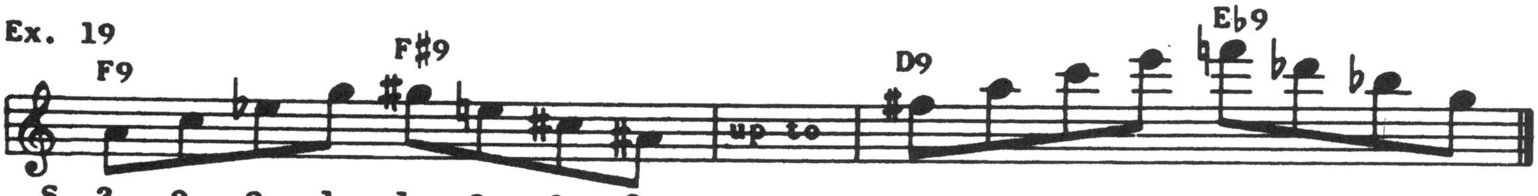

F9
F♯9
up to
D9
E♭9

S.	3	2	2	1	1	2	2	3
F.	2	1	4	3	3	4	1	2

Ex. 20

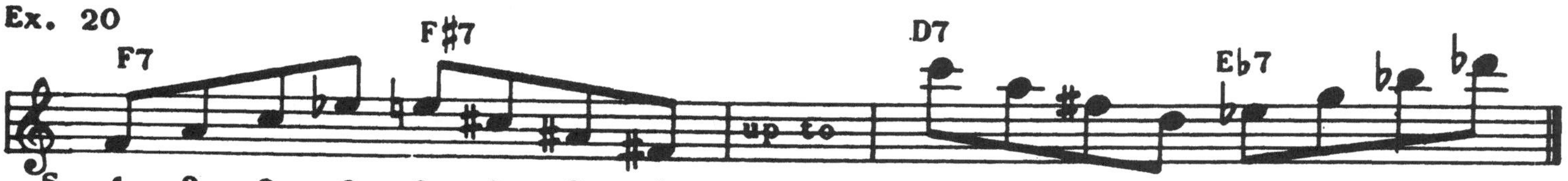

F7
F♯7
up to
D7
E♭7

S.	4	3	2	2	2	2	3	4
F.	3	2	1	4	4	1	2	3

Ex. 21

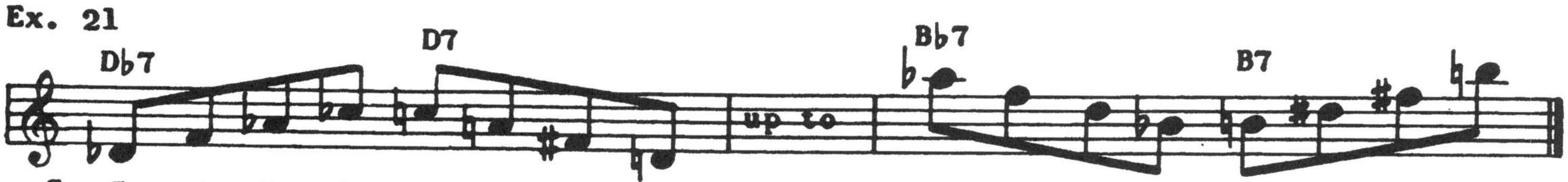

D♭7
D7
up to
B♭7
B7

S.	5	4	3	3	3	3	4	5
F.	4	3	1	4	4	1	3	4

Ex. 22

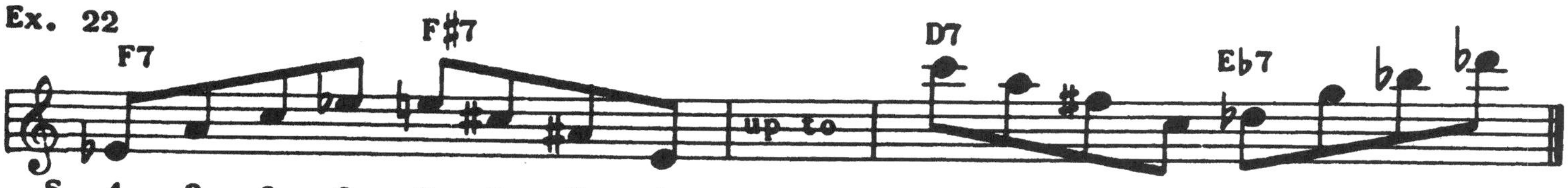

F7
F♯7
up to
D7
E♭7

S.	4	3	2	2	2	2	3	4
F.	1	2	1	4	4	1	2	1

Ex. 23

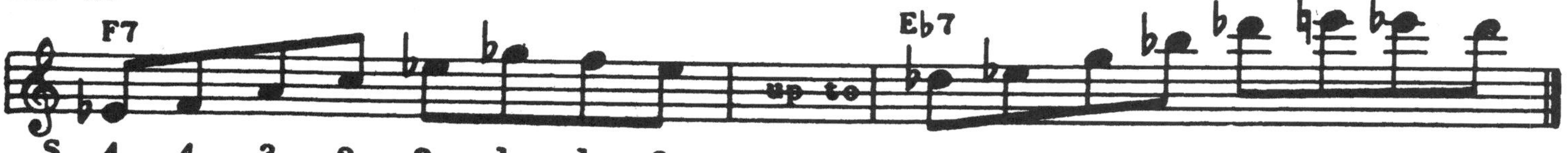

F7
up to
E♭7

S.	4	4	3	2	2	1	1	2
F.	1	3	2	1	4	2	1	4

Use the same fingering going up and down the fingerboard.

LESSON 30
DIMINISHED RUNS

G DIM. GOING UP THE FINGERBOARD

G DIM. GOING DOWN THE FINGERBOARD

LESSON 31

Now that you have your key runs in your head, – of course, I know that you haven't mastered them yet, but you should at least know where to find any run that I tell you to. And if you can't find these runs every place on your guitar, you're not ready for this lesson.

The Blues play a very important part in modern jazz, so we are going to start our solo work with blues patterns.

The keys that the blues are played in mostly, are: – F, G, A♭, B♭ and C. So these are the keys that you are to concentrate on for now. These simple patterns that I have written out in the next few lessons are to be transposed to all five of these keys. Now I am using these runs just as they were in the exercise, so all you have to do is to find the right one.

BLUES No. 1

BLUES No. 2

BLUES No. 3

LESSON 32

In this Lesson we are going to analyze Lesson No. 31.

I know that a lot of things were done in this Lesson that you don't quite understand, so I want you to review Lesson No. 31 and No. 32 over and over again as time goes by, because anything that you don't understand now will become clear as you go farther in the book.

Blues *No. I*:—

In Blues No. I for the first four bars I'm using an Emi7 run. You know that the chord for these four bars are G major for three and G7 for one. But Emi7 and Gma6 are the same (relatives), so it can be used as a major run (See Lesson 19). The same rule that applies to chords applies to runs. In the fifth and sixth bars we're using a Gmi7 run. You know of course, that a Gmi7 run can be used against a C7 chord (See Lesson No. 12). The seventh and eighth bars go back to Emi7.

Now we have one Bar of Ami7 and one bar of Gmi7 in our ninth and tenth measure. In Blues progression sometimes at the ninth and tenth bar we use the V7 for one bar (which is D7 in the key of G major), and the IV7 for one bar (which is C7 in the key of G major), this allows you to use an Ami7 run for one bar and a Gmi7 run for one bar.

A good way to get a better understanding of this is to play the chord progressions to the Blues, and when you get to the ninth and tenth bars, play one bar of Ami7, Ami6, and one bar of Gmi7, Gmi6 — (That's in the key of G major). Keep practicing this progression. Learn to recognize it when you hear it. The last two bars go back to Emi7.

Blues *No. II*:—

Now in Blues No. 2 we start out using our Emi7 run again for the first three bars and at the fourth bar we use a G9th run which is good because there is a G7 chord. The 5th and 6th bars back to Gmi7 run, 7th and 8th bars back to Emi7 run. Now we come to the last four bars. In the 9th and 10th bars we have two bars of D7, but I'm using an Ami7 run for one bar and a Cmi7 run for one bar. Now this is something that can be done in any song blues, ballad, or bounce tune. Go back to Lesson No. 16. Now look at Dom. to Maj. chord connections. Notice that when connecting a dominant chord to a major the dominant in most of the time altered, (G7♯5♭9 to Cma or G13♭5♭9 to Cma). By altering chords like this they blend together perfectly. This same thing applies to solo work. Whenever you have one or two bars of D7 going into G major, you may use an Ami7 run to a Cmi7 run which will blend right into a G major run. In the last two bars we have a Bmi7 run which is a relative to Gma7. Bmi7 and Gma7 are such close relatives that one can be used for the other at any time.

Blues *No. III*:—

Now in Blues No. 3 the first eight bars are like the other's. The 9th and 10th bars have the same idea as in Blues No. 1, and in the last two bars we have what I call a riff run. Riffs can be used any place, but we're not ready to go into riffs yet, so you just accept it for what it is now.

This Lesson is the most important one in this section, because all of those that are to follow will be based on this one. Of course, as you go further in the book things will become more clear to you.

But I want you to go over this Lesson at least three or four times a week, every week. All of this material is in G major and it should be transposed to the keys of: A♭, B♭, C, D♭, E♭ and F major. The best thing to do is to set aside a whole day for each key.

I would like for you to stay with Lessons No. 31, 32 and 33 (which is to follow) for at least a month.

LESSON 33

In this Lesson you are going to work out some ideas for yourself. I want you to take the same runs that we have in Blues No. 1, 2 and 3. Then change them around in as many different ways as you can possily think of, just as I have done.

You should be able to make up at least three more solos for each one of these blue examples. Remember now to use every trick that's possible. There are many, many ways to switch these runs around. The harder you work on it the easier it becomes, and that's when you start getting ideas.

I'd rather you work out all of your ideas in G major first, then transpose them to all of the other keys.

I hope that you are following my instructions as accurately as possible, because I'm not going to take time to explain every little thing as we go further on in the book.

LESSON 34

We will work out some new runs this week which are also taken from your runs in Lesson 28 to 30.

As you practice these runs take notice to how closely related they are to those that we've been working with.

As you can see, these runs are to be played chromatically always up the finger board and back down again.

MAJOR, MINOR AND DOMINANT RUNS

Run No. 3 Fmi7 Run
F♯mi7 Run
up to
Dmi7 Run
S. 4 4 3 2 2 1 1
F. 2 3 1 1 4 3 1

Run No. 4 Fmi7 Run
F♯mi Run
up to
Dmi Run
S. 4 3 2 2 3 2 1 1
F. 3 1 3 1 3 1 3 1

Run No. 5
A♭7♯9 Run
A7♯9 Run
up to
F7♯ Run
S. 4 4 4 3 3 3 3 4
F. 1 3 4 1 4 2 1 4

Run No. 6
D7 Run
3
E♭7 Run
3
up to
B♭7 Run
3
S. 3 3 3 3 4 4 3 3 2
F. 4 3 2 1 4 3 1 4 3

LESSON 35

Now you have a lot of runs to work with, but you don't know how to connect them, so in this Lesson I have worked out some of the most important run connections.

As we go on with our studying these connections will keep appearing from time to time, so work them out as they are, then work them out chromatically, always up and down the finger board.

Notice that over the top of each run I have the chords (like D7 to G major), and below I have the runs that can always be used against these chord progressions.

After you've learned the connections by heart, practice strumming the chords and humming the runs to yourself. By doing this, you can hear just how these runs sound against the chord progressions. Then take the same runs and try to make new ideas.

All you have to do is to use different tempos, and timings, and you will get new effects.

RUN CONNECTIONS
(Dominant To Major Runs In G Major)

LESSON 36

In Lesson No. 35 we worked out run connections.

In this Lesson we put these connections to work. I have written out a Blues solo using most of the runs that we were working with.

This solo is in the key of G major, and should be played between the 7th and 12th frets on your guitar. With this information you should very easily find the proper fingering.

After you work this solo out in G major, transpose it to the keys of D♭, E♭, F, A♭ and B♭.
In each of these keys you are to use the *same fingering*. You only change the position.

BLUES SOLO

Bounce tempo
Gma Run
3
Dim. Run
3
C7 Run
Gma Run
Bmi
B♭mi
Ami
3
Ami Run
B7 Run
G7 Run
C7 Run
Gma Run
Ami Run
3
3

LESSON 37

By now you should know every one of these runs in all keys, and the same is true for the solos.

If you have followed my instructions to the letter, you should have a good knowledge of your instrument from the first up to the 12th fret. If you haven't advanced this far, the best thing to do is to go back to Lesson 24 and start all over again.

We have done a lot with blues progressions up to this point (of course, there is a lot more to be done later on in the book), so we will close this study for a while and go into something else.

But first, we will work out one more study in Blues. In this solo we have four choruses of the Blues. I'm writing out the first chorus and in the next three choruses, I'm leaving it up to you to fill in some of the runs.

If you will notice I've written two or three bars, and in some places the bars are blank. This of course is where you fill in. Over these blank bars I have written the type of run I'd like for you to use, so all you have to do is fill them in.

Don't use these runs just as I have them written. Change them around in as many ways as you can. Keep striving for new ideas.

Another thing — when you work this solo out in G major, transpose it to: F, A♭, B♭, and C. Above all, don't just throw the runs together. Make sure that they blend together as well as those that I have written.

BOUNCE BLUES

Gma Run
Gma Run
G9 Run
Gmi Run
G♯dim Run
Gma Riff
S.2 1 2 2 1 2 2 3 3 3 2 2 1 1
F.1 3 1 1 3 1 1 3 1 2 1 3 1 1
Gma Riff
G♯dim Run
C7 Run
C9 Run
Gma Riff
S.2 1 2 3
F.1 2 4 1 4 1 4 2 1 4 1 4 3
3
Gma Riff
S.3 4
F.1 4 1 4
"Play a four bar blues idea here"
Ami7 Run
D7♯9 Run
Gma Run

LESSON 38

So we have worked with blues progressions and made solos from them.

Now we will work with Vamp changes. But before we go into that let's analyze Lesson 37. You know about everything in this Lesson except the "Riff Runs" Riff runs can be used in most any song if you know where to use them. In some songs you can use them most any place in the song, while in others there are given places.

In Lesson 37 I have them placed in the best places to get the effect that I want you to get. Riff Runs are only ideas put together and forced against the chord. They don't have to be true to the chord.

Take the first three bars of Lesson No. 37. You know that the chords there are all G major but I'm using a rift here which has tones in it that are not Major at all, yet it fits against the chords. We are going to do a lot of work with riff runs from here on out, so anything that you don't understand now about riffs will come as we go on.

In this Lesson I have written out a few riffs that we will be using in the next few lessons.

RIFF RUNS IN G MAJOR

Bounce

No.5
S. 2 2 1-2 1 2 1
F. 1 3 1-1 1 3 4 1 3 1
No.6
S. 2 1 2 1-2 2 4 3 3
F. 3 1 3 2 1 1-1 1 3 1 2
No.7
S. 3 3 2 3 1 2 3 2 1 2 3
F. 1 3 2 3 1 2 3 2 1 2 3
No.8
S. 3 2 3 2
F. 2 1 3 4 3 1 2 1 3 1
No.9
S. 3 3 2 1 1 2 3 2 3 2
F. 1 3 1 3 4 1 3 1 2 1 4 3 1 2 1 3 1 2 1 3
No.10
S. 1 2 3 4 3
F. 1 4 2 1 2 1 4 2 1 3 4 3 1 4 3 1 3 1
No.11
S. 2 3 3 2 2 2 1
F. 2 1 3 1 2 4 1 2 4
No.12
S. 3 3 2 2 1 3 3 2 2 2 3
F. 1 3 2 2 1 2 3 4 1 1 1 2 3 4 2 2 4 3 2 1

LESSON 39

Now we are back to the Vamps again. You know that you studied Vamp chord progressions in Lesson No. 13 and 14.

So now, you're going to fit solos against the chord progressions. This is where riffs get the most use. The chord changes in Vamps move a little too fast for us to use chord runs, so we have to run ideas, which is where riffs come in.

In this Lesson I am going to write out a few 8 bar Vamp solos in G major, and I'm only using the riffs that you had in Lesson No. 38. This is what I want you to do. Learn them all by heart, keep practicing them until you can sing them as you play them. Once you can sing them to yourself, try playing the chord progressions and singing the riffs together. Play the progressions as I have them written out in Lesson No. 14, as you sing the riffs. Keep doing this every day until you can feel yourself getting in a groove with these riffs. If you do this continually they will become a part of you, and you will begin to feel them, and know where to use them. This will also develop the ear. After you have done this for a few days try making up new ideas from these. Try singing new ideas as you play the chord progressions.

I'm not putting the fingering under these notes, because you should know exactly where to find, and how to finger these riffs.

After you have worked these 8 bar Vamps out in G major, you are to do the same in the keys of: F, A♭, B♭, C, D♭ and E♭.

Remember, you are not to rush through this material. Take your time and do it all right.

VAMP RIFFS

No.3
Gma7 Gma6 Ami7 Ami6 Bmi7 B♭mi7 Ami7 D13♭5♭9
Gma7 G13 Cma6 C♯dim Dma6 Emi7 Ami7 D13♭5♭9
No.4
Gma6 C♯dim Cma6 C♯dim Gma7 C♯dim Cma6 C♯dim
Gma6 G13 Cma6 C♯dim Dma6 Emi7 Ami7 D13♭5♭9
No.5
Gma6 C♯dim Cma6 C♯dim Gma6 D13♭9
Gma6 C♭dim Cma6 C♯dim Gma6 D13♭9
No.6
Gma6 C♯dim Cma6 C♯dim Gma6 C♯dim Cma6 C♯dim
Gma7 G13 Cma6 C♯dim Dma6 Emi7 Ami7 D7♯5♭9

LESSON 40

Now we are back to bridges (See Lesson No. 15).

We're going to work out solos or chord runs to fit those bridges we had in Lesson No. 15. These are the most used in Vamps and modern Jazz tunes. This will be easy for you because you can run your chords.

Go back to Lesson No. 29! Here you have dominant chord runs that can be worked right into these bridges. We can't use them as they are, but if we build around them and create a few ideas we can come up with some nice solos.

I have worked out six 8 bar solos in this Lesson. You are to learn them as they are first, and then work out new ones from them.

In Lesson No. 15 those bridges are for the key of C major, but I'm writing these solos out for the key of G major, because that's the key that we have been doing all of our solos work in.

By the way, that run at the end of each 8 bar bridges is going into a G major chord; that's why the last two bars are written like they are.
If you can't find the fingering and the strings that these solos are written for, you are not ready for this Lesson. You should go back to Lesson No. 24 and start all over again.

BRIDGES
(In The Key Of G Major)

No. 1

Bounce tempo
B7 Run
B7
B7
Bmi Run
E7
E7
A7 Run
A7
A7
D7
Ami Run
D7
Cmi Run

No. 2

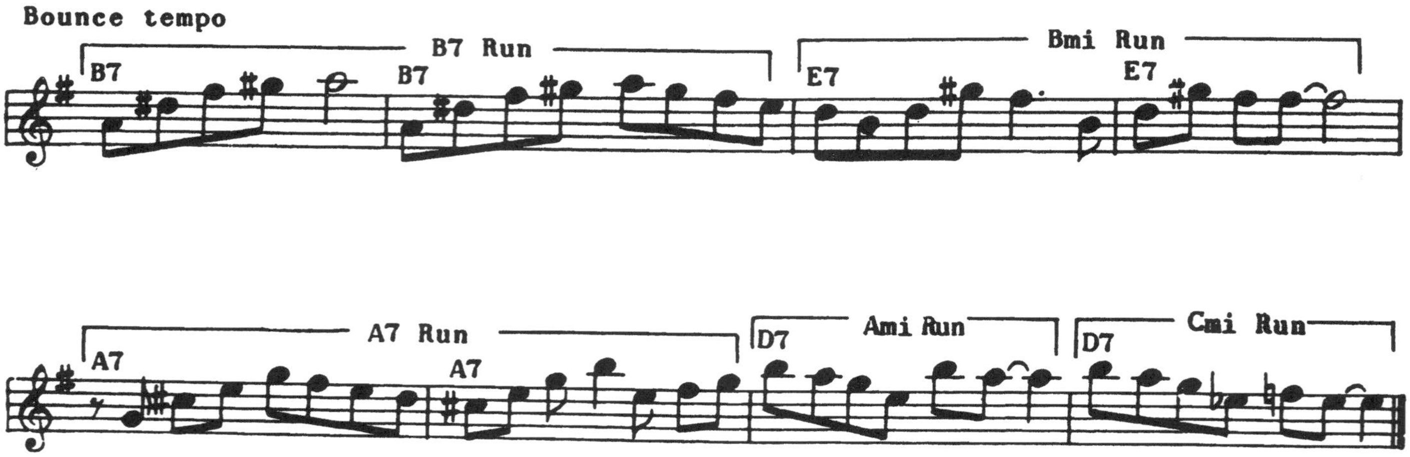

B7 Run
B7
B7
Bmi Run
E7
E7
A7 Run
A7
A7
D7
Ami Run
D7♯9 Run
D7

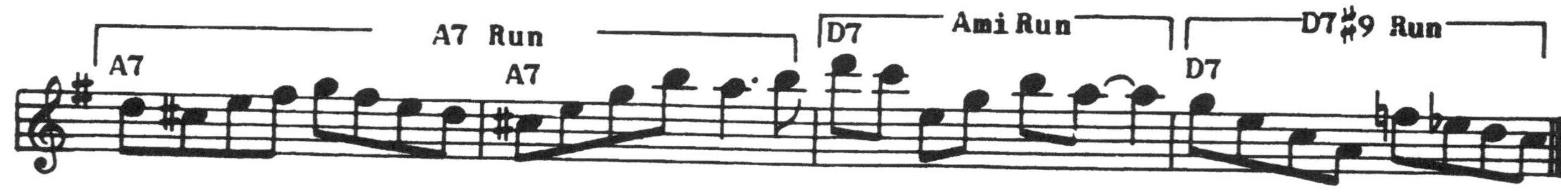

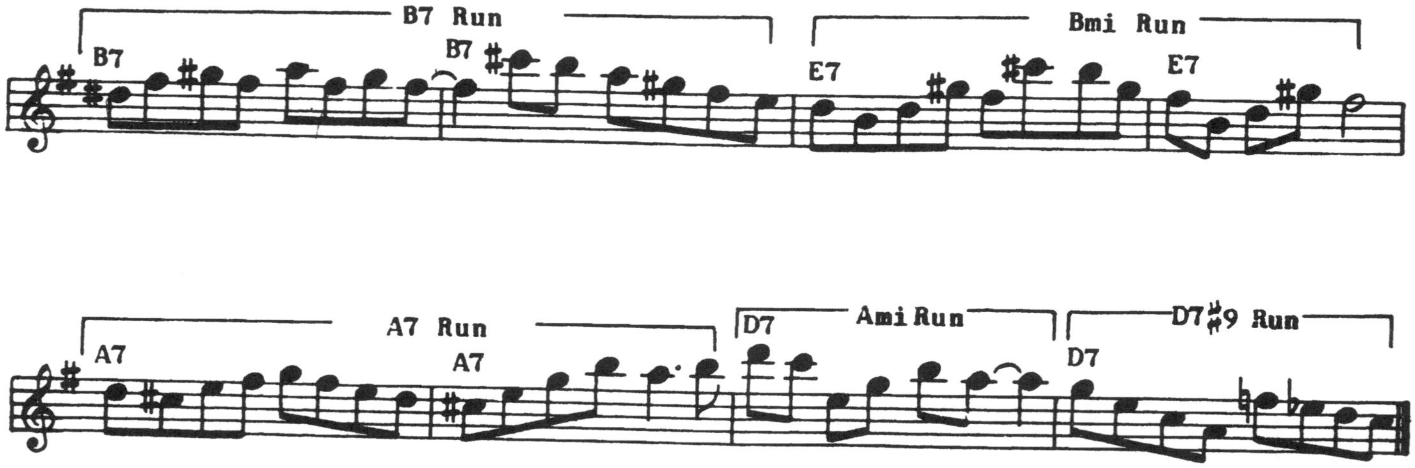

No.3
Dmi Run
G7
Fmi Run
G7
Cma Riff
C
C
A7 Run
A7
A7
Ami Run
D7
D7
No.4
G7 Run
G7
G7
A7 Run
A7
A7
D7 Riff
D7
D7
No.5
B7 Run
B7
B7
Emi Run
Emi
Emi
Emi Run
A7
A7
Ami Run
D7
D7♯9 Run
D7
No.6
B7 Run
B7
B7
Emi Run
Emi
Emi
Em Run
A7
A7
D7 Riff
D7
D7

LESSON 41

This Lesson is going to require a lot of practicing and writing on your part!

First, I want you to practice those riffs in Lesson No. 38 chromatically always up and down the fingerboard. Then you are to write them out in the keys of: F, A^b, B^b, C, D^b, and E^b. This must be done to have a record of these riffs in all of the Jazz keys. (We are going to leave the key of G major soon and if you have these riffs written out in all of the other keys, you won't have any trouble). This is going to call for a lot of transposing, but if you have followed my instructions up to this point, you should not have any difficulty. I would like for you to stay on Lessons No. 38 to 42 for about two months. I want you to play these riffs in any key without any difficulty, and know the fingering and timing. Also to make up new ideas from those that you have.

Don't forget what I told you in Part 2 of this book. Use every trick you can think of to get new ideas.

You can see that I have set aside two positions for each key. In Lesson No. 38, you have six riff runs in one position and six in still another position. The first six are in what is known as the 3rd position, because your first finger falls behind the 3rd fret on your Guitar. The 2nd six are in the 7th position, because your first finger falls behind the 7th fret on your Guitar. In other words, the fret that your first finger falls behind is the position that you are in. In the key of G major, the 3rd and 7th positions are the most important in that key. In the key of Ab major it would be the 4th and 8th positions, in B^b major the 6th and 10th positions and so on. Now, when we get to the key of C major, we can use the 8th position, but we can't use the 12th position, because it is too far up on the fingerboard. So, this means that in the key of C major we only have one position for riff runs which is the 8th position. The key of D^b, and E^b are O.K. because we can get both positions. In D^b at the 1st and 9th positions and in E^b maj. at the 3rd and 11th positions.

When you write out those riffs in Lesson 38 don't forget to write them in the position that I have suggested.

Now you know two positions for each key and you should be able to play these riffs in both positions in all keys. As we go on with our studying you will find that these are the two most important positions, for solo work in each key. There are other positions that we will work with, but they are not as important. So we will concentrate on these for now.

Just as it was with chords it is also with solo work. Having set positions to take solos from makes things so much easier. You always know where to start and end your solos at.

LESSON 42

I know that these bridge solos in Lesson No. 40 were pretty technical, but remember, — all of this material is to be played with an up and down stroke, right from Lesson No. 24 up to this point. If you have any difficulty with your technique, go back to Lesson No. 24 and study it. Remember what I said about up and down strokes. If some of these runs have too many notes in them for you, break them down, use less notes, and play them a little slower.

Let us analyze Lesson No. 40. You will notice that in some places where we have dominant chords I am using minor runs. You know that the 5th of a dominant chord can be substituted in the dominant place, because they are closely related, (See Lessons No. 12 and 32). In bridge No. 1 of Lesson No. 40 the 3rd and 4th bars are E7th, but we are using another Bmi run at this point. In still other places I'm using riff runs which you are familiar with, and the last two bars of each bridge you worked with in run connections (Lesson No. 35), so you should understand what I have done well enough to go into deeper study.

Now you have three different bridges with two solos for each. I want you to make up two more solos for each bridge . . . Using the same runs that I've used; that is, where I have 7th runs you are to use 7th runs. Where I have minor runs you use minor runs. The same holds true for the riffs. I want you to duplicate each bar with the same kind of run. But! You have to change them around. Take each run and play it in as many ways as you can to get a different sound — do as much as you can to get a new effect. One good way to do this is to learn all of the solos by heart. Then sing them as you play the chords. This will help you to feel the run, and also give you a better idea of what they sound like against the chords (See Lesson No. 39).

After you have done this, you are to transpose all of them to the keys of: F, A♭, and B♭ major. These are the keys that they are used in most.

In fact, as you continue to play Jazz you will find that most of your jump tunes such as "The Blues, Vamps, and Novelty tunes" that employ this type of bridge are in the keys of: F, G, A♭, B♭, and C major. Don't leave this Lesson until you have done all of this work.

LESSON 43

Now we are up to what we call Rhythm changes.

Rhythm changes are pretty much the same as Vamps. The only difference is this, when a musician says let's play some rhythm changes they are always in B♭ major (concert).

I can go so far as to say that every Jazz Musician ever to have a name, has recorded these changes over and over again, and every musician that has ever owned an instrument has played them hundreds of times. So you can see just how important rhythm changes are.

In this Lesson I have written out the chord changes that are best in most cases (at least, the ones that I use the most), and a solo. Work out the chord progressions first, then analyze the solo. In the solo I am using the riffs that we had in Lesson No. 38.

Notice that I have four bars of written-out solos, and four blank bars. You are to fill in the blank bars with a riff, (like you did in Lesson No. 37). You can use the riffs that we had in Lesson No. 38, or you can make up new ones. Just make sure that they blend together smoothly like those that I have written out.

After you have worked out riffs for the whole solo, try some more riffs in these same places. Make up at least four riffs for each blank space that I have in this solo.

RHYTHM CHANGES

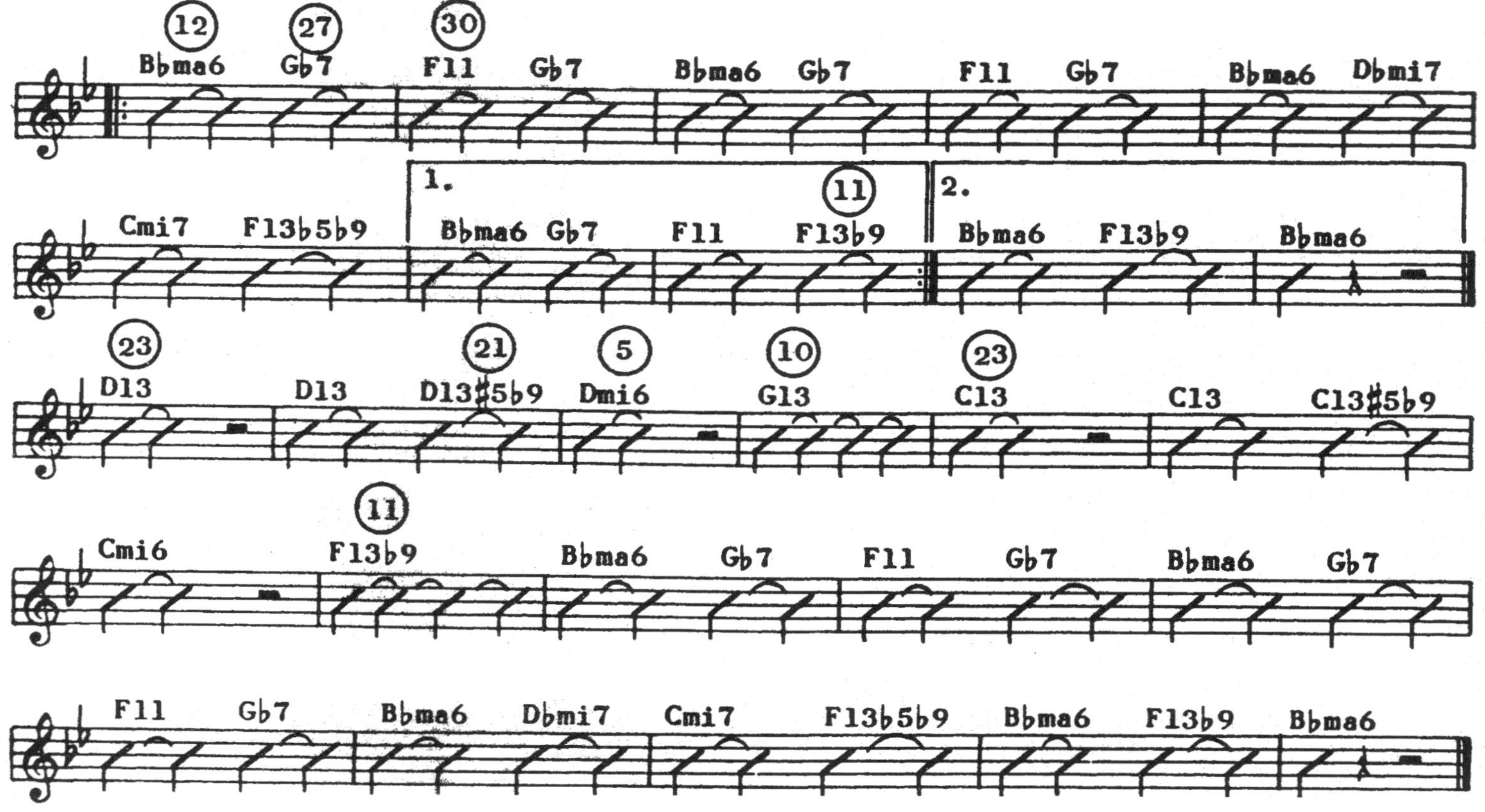

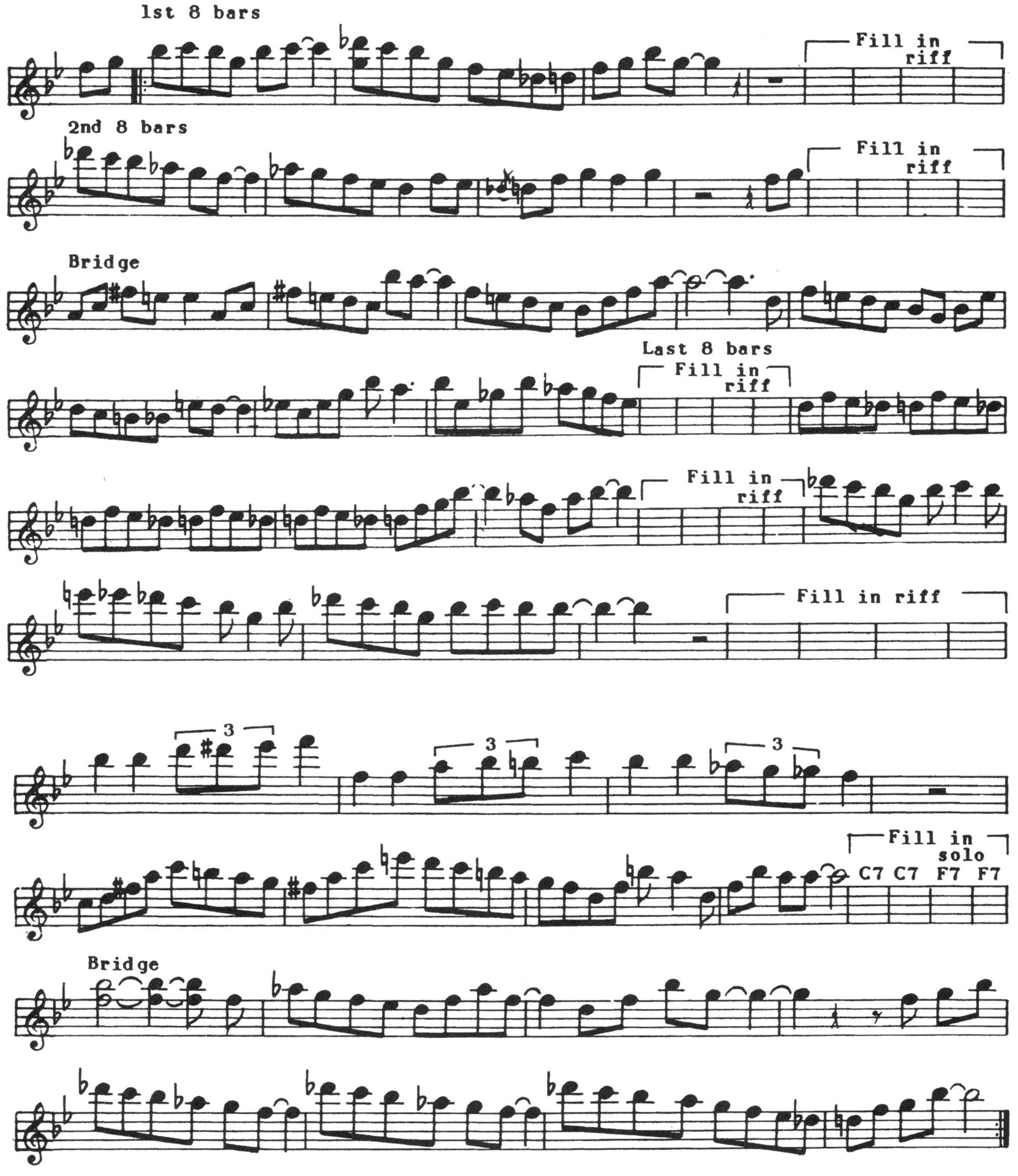
1st 8 bars
Fill in riff
2nd 8 bars
Fill in riff
Bridge
Last 8 bars
Fill in riff
Fill in riff
Fill in riff
3
3
3
Fill in solo
C7 C7 F7 F7
Bridge

LESSON 44

Well, you should be coming along nicely by now.

If you have followed my instructions to the letter you've been studying in this book almost a year now, and I know that you have gained a lot of musical knowledge. Ideas should be coming to you much easier now than they were before you started this study.

We are going to work out one more study in rhythm changes, then we will leave them for good. You are going to take all of your riffs in Lesson No. 39, and all of your bridges in Lesson No. 40, plus all of the new ideas that you have worked out from them, — then you are to make up six rhythm solos using each of these bridges in Lesson No. 40. This will give you three different types of rhythm solos, which will be of great benefit to you as you advance further.

Write them out on manuscript paper for future references. By continually writing out this material like this, you gain a wider musical knowledge, and it helps your reading ability tremendously.

After you have written them out in B♭ major, transpose them to the keys of: F, G, A♭ and C major.

LESSON 45

Well, we have worked with Vamps, bridges, the Blues, and you know how to use runs in all keys.

Now we are coming to what I call the grand finish. These last few lessons are going to deal with everything that you have learned, throughout the course.

In this Lesson I have written out solo sketches for those 8 bar sequences in Lesson No. 23. If you will remember I told you that these were some of the most used chord progressions in modern Jazz. So I am giving you a few ideas on how to build solos around them.

I have them arranged just as they were in Lesson No. 23, 8 bar solos for each sequence from No. 1 up to No. 7. Work out each solo to itself. Then analyze it, take close notice as to how I connect my runs.

Every run connection that appears here has been used at one time or another in your studies, so you should have no trouble finding the right fingering for them.

Just take your time and work out each sequence slowly. After you have done this, make up at least two 8 bar solos for each sequence, then transpose them to all of the other keys, just as you did in Lesson No. 23.

No.3
C7 Run
Bb7 Run
Eb Riff
No.4
Gmi Run
Fma Riff
No.5
Gmi Riff
Dim. Riff
No.6
Eb7 Run
Ab Run
Bbmi Run
Dbmi Run
Ab Riff
No.7
Bb Riff
C7 Run
F7 Run
Bbma Run

LESSON 46

We are still working with those sequences in Lesson No. 23. Only this time we will work out solos for the 16 bar sequences, (No. 8 to 11).

This is to be done the same way as you did Lesson No. 45. Work out each solo, analyze it. Then make up two more solos for each sequence, and transpose them to all of the other keys.

No.10
F7 Run
Bb7 Run
Eb7 Run
Ab Riff
C7 Run
No.11
F Run
Ami Run
G7 Run
Gmi Run
F7 Run
Bb Run
Bbmi Run
F Riff
G7 Run
Gmi Run

LESSON 47

Before we go into this study, let's go back to Lesson No. 45 and 46.

If you will notice, a lot of places in those solos I am using riffs, while the chord changes for these measures are completely foreign to the riff itself (See Lesson No. 38). But I have forced the riffs against the progressions.

In order to get a better understanding of this, study the riffs in each solo, then the chord progressions for those measures. Then sing the riffs while you play the chord progressions. This way you can hear just how the riffs sound against the chords. Now, in your solos that you made for the sequences, I want you to fit in riffs every place that I have them. See how many of your riffs you can force in, at these places. Try to fit in all of your riffs from Lesson No. 38.

I am introducing a new position for solo work. This position is to be used for the keys of: A♭, B♭, C, D♭, and E♭ major (it can be used for F, and G major but it is a little out of range). I have written out a few riffs in this new position to show where to find it. But in order to really get that position under your fingers, I want you to take all of your riffs in Lesson No. 38 and transpose them to this key. Then work them out in this position. After you have done this, work them out in all of the other keys.

These riffs are in the key of B♭ major and this position extends from the 3rd to the 6th frets on your Guitar.

RIFFS IN B♭ MAJOR
(In The 3rd Position)

LESSON 48

In this Lesson I am introducing the groove riff.

When you go through this solo that I have written out, you will find that the first and the last courses are the same. This is known as a groove riff. Groove riffs are repeated consecutively.

If you will notice, in the first and last 12 bars I am using the same run over and over again. That's the way this type of riff is used. No doubt you've heard Jazz combos play riffs like this many times before they went into their solo. You usually start and end a song with groove riffs. These kind of riffs are only used against Blues and vamp changes (progression).

This solo is in the key of B♭ major and it employs some of the riffs in Lesson No. 47, along with a few new ones. Now the tricky part about this solo is that it's all done in the 3rd position on your Guitar (between the 3rd and 6th frets).

Another thing is that most of all the runs that I am using are riff runs. Take close notice to how I force the riffs against the chords progressions. I would like for you to practice this solo until you can sing it by heart. Then when you can sing it, play the chord progressions as you sing, so you can hear how the riffs sound against the chords.

GROOVE RIFFS
(In B♭ Major)

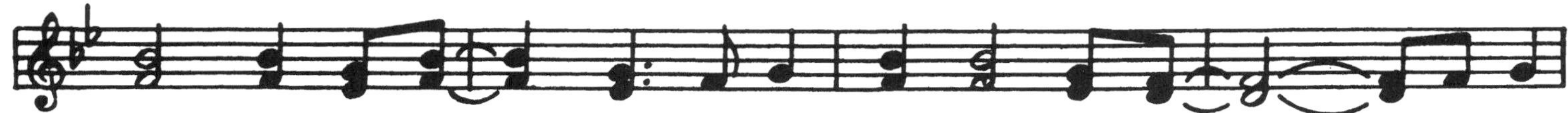

LESSON 49

Now you have some real work to do! First, take your solo in Lesson No. 48, and write it out in the keys of: A♭, C, D♭, and E♭ major, then practice it in all of these new keys. Try devoting at least one full day to each key. After you can play this solo in all of these keys, I want you to make up two more four course solos. Start and end each course with a groove riff, as I have done.

If you have a hard time trying to make up groove riffs, take your Guitar and play the chord progressions to the Blues, and start singing any of your riffs, and keep singing them until you can get one that fits in the 12 bar sequence three times, as well as the one in Lesson No. 48. It may take a little time to get a good groove on these riffs, but remember, practice makes perfect, and if you practice this material long enough and hard enough, you will surely begin to feel it.

That's why I always tell you to go back over these lessons so much, because I know that every time you review a lesson, you will learn something new about it. You see, when you are studying from a book like this, you're limited from the beginning because you don't have a teacher there to explain everything to you. This means that you are going to have to study like a madman to really learn anything. So keep reviewing these lessons, even after you have gone through the entire book.

LESSON 50

Well, we have worked with just about everything, except building around melodies, so this is what we will end our studies with.

In this Lesson we have an old folk song "Dark Eyes". I suppose you know it — most everyone does! I have the sample melody written out for the first course, and in the remaining courses I'm building around the melody. Play this solo slowly and make it as effective as possible. Go over it consecutively until you know it by heart. Notice how you can always hear the melody though it's not really there.

I want you to make up a solo with this song, and build around the melody as I have done. All you have to do is run chords around it. Keep playing the melody and trying to fit in chord runs until you get some ideas.

You only have three chords to worry about. That is, A7, Dmi and Gmi. Make up at least four courses. By the way, this solo is in the 5th position and in the key of Dmi. You are to write it out in the keys Cmi, E♭mi, and Fmi.

BUILDING AROUND THE MELODY
("DARK EYES" In D Minor)

LESSON 51

This Lesson is to be worked out the same way as you did last week's lesson.

Your chords are E7 Ami, and Gmi, and the song is in the key of A minor. I am using the same melody (Dark Eyes), because it is easy to build solos around.

Every note in this solo is between the 7th and 11th frets on your Guitar (the 7th position). You are not to leave this position to play any part of this solo. Other than that, just follow the same rules of Lesson No. 50.

After you have worked out and analyzed this solo, make up a four course solo, using these same ideas, and in this same position. Then transpose both this and your solo to the keys of: B♭mi, Fmi, and Gmi.

BUILDING AROUND THE MELODY (Cont.)
("DARK EYES" In A Minor)

3
3
3
3
3
3

LESSON 52

In this your last Lesson, I have written out six examples on how to build around a melody. Each of these examples are in different keys, and there are two four bar praises to each one. The four bar praises at the top of each example give you the melody and the chord progressions. The praise at the bottom gives you the solo built around the melody.

I have also used different types of melodies and chord progressions for each one. This is done to give you an idea on how to build solos around melodies with various types of chord progressions. Now you are to learn the melody to each example first. Keep strumming the chords and humming the melody until you know it by heart. Then practice the solo. All of the runs in these solos are those that you have had before in other lessons, only the timing is a little different. So you should be able to find them without difficulty.

After you have practiced each of these examples you will notice that the melody can be heard in every solo, even though it is not there. Now to build solos around melodies like this is not an easy thing to do. You will have to work very hard. What you have to do is learn to make up patterns.

Let's go back to Lessons No. 50 and 51. Here in each course of these solos I have set a different solo pattern, and I keep that pattern going throughout the solo. Now go over each solo with the thought of patterns in mind. You can see that although the runs are different from one another, they follow the same pattern. Now look at this week's Lesson. Take Example No. 1; in the first bar of the solo we have one quarter note, four sixteenth notes and three quarter triplets (lazy triplets). In the second bar you have the same identical timing, only the run is different. In the 3rd and 4th bars we are still using the same pattern with a different run, of course. Everything in the solo followed the pattern that I set at the beginning. Look at the rest of your examples. Notice how the first measure sets the pattern for all of the measures to follow. This is what we call solo patterns. After you have studied this Lesson and learned each solo, you are to make up two solo patterns for each example. Then transpose every example to all of the other keys. When you come across chord progressions similar to these, you will always have them to refer to, for solo patterns.

SOLO PATTERNS

B♭ B♭ma7 Cmi7 Cmi6 Cmi7 Cmi6 Cmi7 Cmi6
Gma7 Gma6 Gma7 Gma6 Bmi7 B♭mi7 Ami7 Ami6
G7 C7 F D7
E♭ E♭dim Fmi Ddim
E♭mi B♭7 E♭mi A♭7 D♭ma7 E♭mi Fmi B♭7°